# THE
# URANUS-NEPTUNE
# INFLUENCE

D1553599

# THE URANUS-NEPTUNE INFLUENCE

## JOY MICHAUD

SAMUEL WEISER, INC.

York Beach, Maine

First published in 1994 by
Samuel Weiser, Inc.
P. O. Box 612
York Beach, ME 03910-0612

Library of Congress Cataloging-in-Publication Data
Michaud, Joy
    The Uranus-Neptune influence / by Joy Michaud.
      p.  cm.
    Includes bibliographical references and index.
    1. Astrology. 2. Uranus (Planet)—Miscellanea.
    3. Neptune (Planet—Miscellanea.   I. Title.
    BF1724.2.U7M53 1994
    133.5'3--dc20                94-16827
ISBN 0-87728-806-2                CIP
MG

Cover illustration, *The Quest,* and illustrations on pages xx,
xxi, 65, 67, 68, 98, 138, 146 are copyright © 1994 Erich
Holmann. Used by kind permission of the artist.

Typeset in 11 point Perpetua

Printed in the United States of America

99 98 97 96 95 94
10 9 8 7 6 5 4 3 2 1

The paper used in this publication meets the minimum require-
ments of the American National Standard for Permanence of
Paper for Printed Library Materials Z39.48-1984.

# TABLE OF CONTENTS

> The effects of the transpersonal planets on our personal reality; how to begin to understand their influence in world and universal terms.

> Neptune in mythology as Poseidon—son of Saturn and grandson of Uranus; his identity within other creeds and cultures. Music and poetry inspired by Neptunian influences.

> A general look at the planet Neptune and its place in our solar system. Neptune's personal placement in each house; how Neptune affects generations.

> A basic interpretation of Neptune's effects. A case history indicating a strong Neptune influence.

> Showing the highest as well as the lowest manifestations of the Neptune influence.

Uranus depicted as heaven, the "heavenly man," or "creative will." Husband of Gaia the Earth, and father of Saturn. A close look into the myths and legends surrounding this god, as well as his identity in the mythology of differing cultures past and present.

A general look at the planet Uranus and its place in our solar system. Uranus' personal placement in each house; the sign Uranus falls in effecting those born during the seven year period when Uranus occupies the sign.

An overall look at Uranus and his force for freedom. Some case histories.

The positive influence of Uranus enables individuals to link together the universal symbols which make up our "reality"; Plato's descriptive explanation of man and his illusions, particularly in regard to earthly existence.

The I Ching; understanding the need for change.

The different ways in which the Uranus force may operate; the Prometheus myth; the relationship of Uranus with the Self.

Questions and answers concerning the meditations; personal
and universal issues discussed.

Saturn, Uranus and Neptune positions from 1900–2000

# CHARTS

# PREFACE

This book investigates the effects of Uranus and Neptune on our human consciousness and condition. However, the text always returns our attention to Saturn, who, as discussed in *The Saturn/Pluto Phenomenon*,[1] is the key to the chart in its entirety. Working to integrate and understand Saturn's effect on our personal psyche can help us identify and release past fears, limitations, and restrictions, as well as giving a greater realization of Self. Saturn is the point from which strength and balance can start to be identified as well as achieved. However, when we bring Pluto into the equation, a greater understanding and release from past needs and obsessional impulses may be gained. Pluto can ascertain and bring to awareness the struggle between the lower self and the higher Self, and in so doing will often bring to the surface a great wealth of talents and abilities which have long been hidden within the psyche.

We are just leaving behind the Piscean Age, which has been with us for the last two thousand years. The ruler of the Piscean Age is Neptune, and therefore in this volume Neptune is discussed first. Now the world is entering the New Age of Aquarius, ruled by Uranus[2] and, although the basic definition of Uranus may be translated into a need for change and for inventive originality, its deeper meaning cannot be fully grasped or interpreted from just a temporal understanding of this influence.

In ancient mythology, Uranus was symbolically the father of Saturn, and the grandfather of Pluto and Neptune. We have in the past given Saturn, Neptune, and Pluto—as well as many other gods—a human form, and it is thus that they are represented throughout history in art, sculpture, and mythology. But Uranus, known as the *heavenly man*, or *the creative mind of god* was never given form by us as were the other ancient gods. There are virtually no statues or paintings depicting Uranus, and those few that exist only relate his figure to the creation of the world. Therefore Uranus in this volume is depicted in the way the ancients intended—without form—and yet his ancient wisdom is there for us to relearn, and to use as something new, different and unique in this, the New Age of Aquarius which we are just entering.

---

[1] *The Saturn/Pluto Phenomenon* (York Beach, ME: Samuel Weiser, 1993).

[2] Before the discovery of Uranus in 1781, the sign of Aquarius was ruled by Saturn and some astrologers still maintain that Saturn therefore is joint ruler of Aquarius.

I would like to express my gratitude to Elizabeth Kingsley-Rowe for her patience and her invaluable help with the manuscript. Also to Erich Holmann for generously allowing me to use his painting on the cover of this book and his beautiful illustrations to illuminate the text.

# INTRODUCTION

During a period between February 1988 and February 1991, Saturn, Uranus, and Neptune were all in the sign of Capricorn. According to the findings of Neil F. Michelsen[1] this configuration of planets last occurred in Capricorn in 1777 B.C. Neptune first entered Capricorn on January 19, 1984. Four years later, in February 1988, Saturn and Uranus entered the same sign, bringing their influence to bear upon all that Capricorn represents: the world, society and state, economic structures and institutions, ambitious enterprises, governments, and, in particular, the leaders of governments, the heads of corporate institutions and industries. Capricorn represents the full power of the state, and the authority of the monarchy.

Neptune is the planet associated with illusion, confusion, fantasy, universal love, compassion, and can bestow certain visionary qualities that can manifest in both positive and negative form. Neptune in Capricorn may give many a vision of a *new world order*, as well as some of the instability this is likely to bring about.

Saturn's transit through Capricorn—and Capricorn is ruled by Saturn—causes limitation and restriction to all that Capricorn stands for, as well as the need for responsible deeds and accomplishments. While the transits of Uranus supply the impetus to break free from Saturn's and Capricorn's limiting influence, bringing revolt, revolution and breakdown to many different areas of the world and society. On a more positive level, this could manifest as new ways to tackle old problems, and new and more humane innovations in medicine and science. The latter of the 20th century also witnessed humankind's breaking of the Earth's limiting influences— one of which is gravity—with the invention and use of spacecraft, space shuttles, modules, probes, and satellites. But the Uranus effect may also signify the terrifying technology used in modern warfare today, which magnifies to a large degree the damage to our globe. Uranus is also representative of satellite and global television, giving us news from every part of Earth. The irony is that a great deal of the news we receive is just more of Neptune's delusion again!

During the period when all three planets occupied Capricorn, there were many major events occurring worldwide. For instance, the radical

---

[1] Neil F. Michelsen, *Tables of Planetary Phenomena* (San Diego, CA: ACS Publications, 1990), p. 88.

changes that took place in the Soviet Union, as well as in other communist countries of Eastern Europe; the Gulf War, following the Iran/Iraq conflict; the problems which flared up between the Serbs, Croats, and Muslims in former Yugoslavia, escalating into a bloody civil war. There was also civil war in Kurdistan, Cambodia, Somalia, Ethiopia and, at the time of writing, an estimated eighty conflicts going on in different parts of the world.

Our world disintegrates before our eyes. We suffer war, see millions dying through famine and, in the West, experience the horrific destruction of much of society by drugs (ruled by Neptune). We also have throughout the world the undermining effect of the AIDS virus: viruses are usually designated as falling under Pluto's rule, but spreading epidemics are associated with Neptune. We have computer games, videos, and virtual reality—Uranian and Neptunian influences combined.

Although Saturn left the sign of Capricorn in February 1991, Uranus and Neptune formed three conjunctions there during 1993. Uranus will leave Capricorn permanently in January 1996; Neptune in November 1998.

The last time Saturn, Uranus, and Neptune were in the same sign was during part of the years 1485-1486[2] when these planets were in the sign of Sagittarius. Chapter 1 explains some of the more positive effects of Saturn, Uranus, and Neptune in Sagittarius, and some of the events, discoveries and changes that resulted from these influences. There were also many famous battles fought and won around this period in history. The Battle of Bosworth (1485) is where Richard III was defeated by Henry Tudor, the first king of the great Tudor dynasty in England. Five years earlier, in 1480, Ivan III liberated Moscow from Mongol rule, declaring himself the first Tsar of Russia; he then rebuilt Moscow over the ensuing years. The conquest of the Moorish kingdom of Granada took place in 1492; here the Christian monarchs, Ferdinand and Isabella, completed the Reconquista.[3] Jews were expelled from the Spanish Kingdoms, and many went to eastern Europe.

The previous time (before the 15th century) when Saturn, Uranus, and Neptune were in the same constellation was in 1307, in the sign of Scorpio. This sign is linked to sex, death, rebirth, the occult, and the arcane. Scorpio can also be a buyer of souls, through envy, desire, and the lust for power.

---

[2] February 15, 1485 to March 31, 1485; October 31, 1485 to January 11, 1486; July 14, 1486 to October 30, 1486. The dates are from *Tables of Planetary Phenomena,* by Neil F. Michelsen, pp. 65, 68, 73.

History books relate that the 14th century was a catastrophic and disastrous time, full of difficulties and setbacks; 1307-1312 was a high point of internal friction and crisis in the church, caused through fateful and calamitous power struggles. Philip IV of France imprisoned the Pope in 1303; he died soon after, and there followed the election of a French Pope, Clement V (1305-1315). In 1306 the Jews were expelled from France, having been expelled from England in 1290 while from 1307-1314 The Order of the Knights Templar[4] was declared heretical, and many knights were tortured and put to death, Pope Clement V being partly responsible for their demise. The Inquisition flourished, but in 1309 Pope Clement fled to Avignon, where the Papacy remained until 1377. The Papal schism took place between 1378 and 1417, with rival Popes, one in Rome and one in Avignon.

Before the discovery of Pluto—now the accepted ruler of Scorpio for most astrologers—in 1930, the sign of Scorpio was ruled by Mars, god of war. It is interesting to note that the first mention of gunpowder being manufactured in Europe dates to circa 1300, while the first canon was invented circa 1313.

Scorpio rules the 8th house, part of which governs others' money and values. In the early 1300s, Edward I standardized certain units of measurement, and introduced the hallmarking of silver articles with the leopard's head, to indicate the Sterling standard in England. Harvest failures and famine in Europe took place from 1315–1317. The Black Death began in 1332, reached Europe in 1347, and killed—between 1347 and 1350—one third of the total population of Europe.

In comparing the two different periods in history and the influences surrounding the combined effects of Saturn, Uranus, and Neptune in any one constellation, a pattern associated with the signs involved seems to emerge, which then affects humanity over the years that follow. What the longterm influence of Saturn, Uranus, and Neptune in Capricorn will be, we must wait and see. The least profitable approach is to contemplate the worst that could happen: we can only hope for the best. Perhaps the most

---

[3] The Reconquista began in the early 11th century. The marriage of Ferdinand of Aragon and Isabella of Castile led to unification of their two kingdoms in 1479. In 1492 they captured Granada, the last Moorish stronghold, and the Christian kingdoms of Spain and Portugal were formed.

[4] A military order of monks, originally founded to protect pilgrims on the crusades.

positive effect that could be envisaged would be an uplifting of consciousness around our globe, taking us into the New Age we are promised. Neptune and Uranus do affect our world and everyday thinking, but because both are transcendental planets, they also initiate states of higher consciousness and awareness.

Understanding the Saturn influence[5] can lead us to greater awareness of the Self, though other planetary influences obviously can also be understood and worked with in a different way. I have tried to devise a psychologically-based system to work with so we can better understand the higher octave planets—Neptune and Uranus—so that they may be more consciously integrated into personality, physical life, and thence into the structures that make up our world.

---

[5] See chapters 7 and 9, also *The Saturn / Pluto Phenomenon*.

*The archetypal images woven together under Neptune's idealistic and illusory influence can symbolize both heaven and hell, and create still more pathways in future existences.*

LE · BATELEUR

VIIII

L'HERMITE

LE · MAT

# NEPTUNE AND URANUS—
# DESTINY AND THE NEW AGE

> Do not seek to have events happen as you want them to, but instead want them to happen as they do happen, and your life will go well.
>
> —Epictetus[1]

In my work as a psychotherapist and astrologer the questions often arise as to the nature of "reality" and "destiny." These two issues have perplexed us from time immemorial, and much of classical philosophical thought is devoted to these questions. If we study astrology and philosophy in the light of modern psychology, we begin to realize that our *reality*, or to use a less questionable word, our *actuality*—how we view the world, what we experience—*is our destiny* unless we learn to reach beyond the illusion of life to that which is the Self. Then free will, and a destiny that is less bound to the wheel of fate can start to become a possibility.

Neptune is the planet most commonly associated with illusion. But illusion itself is a very subtle and elusive thing. Therefore, if we can understand Neptune's role within ourselves in a slightly more objective way, we can put greater trust in Neptune's subjective mode of operation. Uranus, on the other hand, can often indicate a level of intuitive comprehension quite different from the normal human intellect's understanding, and can be invaluable in our search for greater insight and awareness.

In ancient mythology, each planet was represented by a planetary regent or god. If we learn to channel planetary influences by using symbolic

---

[1] *Classics of Western Philosophy*, 3rd edition, ed. Steven M. Cahn (Indianapolis: Hackett Publishing Company, Inc. 1990), p. 327.

imagery—thus working with these gods in a psychological sense—we can begin to understand their purpose and impact on our lives. When we do this, hitherto unconscious psychological forces can become our friends, rather than remaining forces over which we appear to have no control.

It is certain that we all have lessons to learn, and if we can understand what these lessons are, even a difficult planetary cycle can be turned to advantage for our own personal development. The secret is learning how to listen within, having a fervent wish to learn, and cultivating a simplicity toward life that allows the learning process to take place.

It is true many cannot yet integrate the powerful energies of the more transcendental planets, hence our dilemma on all levels of awareness, and the prevalence of many diseases, viruses and mental problems which are as yet little understood. But the new age that we are about to enter will produce many insights and new teachings that encompass all areas of life—physical, mental, emotional, and spiritual. The world as we know it will change dramatically over the next few years and old habits or redundant ways of thinking will no longer serve as they did in the past.

We are just coming to the end of the Piscean Age and entering the Aquarian Age. As we move through the long period of transition between these ages (a period possibly lasting some two or three hundred years), we begin to leave the age which has encompassed two thousand years of Christianity—ironically, perhaps, a dark time characterized by much suffering—to move toward the dawning of a new era, where, hopefully, a more equal and humane society will begin to manifest. Neptune rules Pisces, and Uranus is now the accepted ruler of Aquarius; therefore we should try to use these two planets in unity. Neptune (the mystical) works in harmony with Uranus (the awakener) as the higher aspects of love work in unison with human brotherhood and the Universal Mind—linking the old Piscean Age to the new Age of Aquarius. Within the individual personality, this could manifest as a uniting of Soul and Mind.

Already this integration, working on many different levels of awareness, can be seen to be taking place throughout the world, and will be ever more apparent as we go toward the millennium. Prejudices towards race, religion, sex and sexuality are being broken down. It will eventually be recognized by some that faults lie on both sides, and the oppressed and the oppressor will need to be seen in a clearer context, both personally and collectively. It is not through wishful thinking that this will come about, rather it is inherent in the age and consequent on past karma[2] on a world level.

During a period between 1988 and the beginning of 1991, Saturn, Uranus, and Neptune were all in the sign of Capricorn. This planetary configuration (Saturn, Uranus, and Neptune in the same sign) last occurred five hundred years ago, in the sign of Sagittarius. For a period during 1485-1486, Jupiter (ruler of Sagittarius) and Mars also formed part of this configuration, thus adding expansion and energy to the philosophical and enquiring tendencies already characterized by Sagittarius. (See Chart 1 on page 4.) During that time, all those things relevant to the sign of the Archer were brought to the fore: long journeys and travel—both mental and physical—higher learning, religion, and philosophy.

The latter half of the 15th century was an age of discovery. In 1487, Bartholomeu Diaz sailed around the Cape of Good Hope (South Africa). In 1497, Vasco da Gama found the sea route to India, landing in 1498. On the first of four voyages to the New World, in 1492, Christopher Columbus accidentally discovered the West Indies; and on two subsequent expeditions he reached the South American mainland. Also in 1492, Martin Behaim of Nuremberg constructed the first modern globe, and Leonardo da Vinci designed the first flying machine. These discoveries and inventions expanded our physical and mental horizons, and a great deal of further knowledge was then built upon this foundation.

The 15th century also heralded in the early Renaissance period[3] when the Western European nations began a transition in consciousness. This was partly due to the invention of the first printing press: the printed word became available to many, and much of our surviving philosophical and poetical literature dates from this time. For instance, the first Hebrew bible[4] from which the Christian Bible is derived, was printed in Italy in 1488. The printing of

---

[2] Karma is said to be the Law of Cause and Effect, which is activated by our own unconscious desire nature.

[3] The humanistic revival of classical art, literature, and learning in Europe.

[4] In 1488 the first and possibly the most beautiful of all printed Hebrew bibles was produced in Milan by a family of German Jews. However, this version was revised, and it was the printing shop of a Christian publisher, Daniel Bomberg, that produced the second edition of the Hebrew bible which became the standard printed text. This was published in 1524.

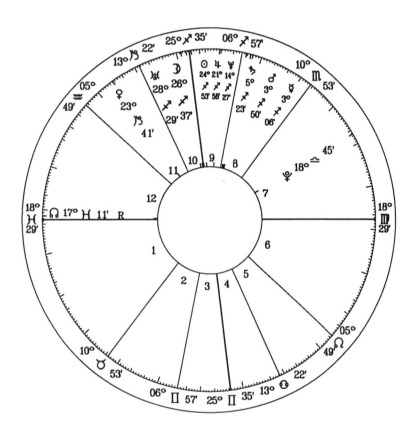

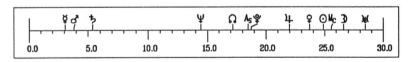

Chart 1. Chart created for 12 noon, December 7, 1485 (O.S.) in London. This imaginary chart has 8 planets in Sagittarius, including Saturn, Uranus and Neptune. Chart calculated by Astrolabe using Nova Printwheels.

music was introduced slightly later, in 1501, by Ottaviani Petrucci in Venice.

It was in 1492 that Lorenzo de' Medici, the last great Medici patron of artists and scholars, died. His family had ruled the city of Florence since 1424, and artistic and intellectual genius had flourished under their patronage. A typical product of his age was Marsilio Ficino (1433-1499), acclaimed as the most important writer of the Italian Renaissance, and high priest of the Florentine Academy. Many acknowledged his work, and thought him the greatest philosopher of the entire Italian Renaissance. It was said he was the inspiration behind many of the great poets, philosophers, artists and statesmen of the time.

Ficino was Master to Pico della Mirandola (1463-1494), accused of heresy but later acquitted. In 1489, Pico wrote *Heptaplus*, a Cabbalistic account of creation. Among his many other works was a treatise against astrology; the gullibility of astrologers was the target of many jests and jokes between Pico and Ficino, but Pico had perhaps misunderstood Ficino's real interest in the subject.

Ficino's *Book of Life* was published in 1489[5] and consisted of three smaller books in one. Book Three in particular caused contention in both Church and State due to the direct reference to the planets and their effect on the human body and temperament. Ficino explained that the gods affected our mind and imagination, rather than causing fatal happenings in our lives, as the astrologers of the day would have it. He began to link ancient astrology to a psychological element virtually unknown at that time.

Ficino's philosophy had as its basis a strong Platonic element[6] that recognized the Soul, and taught that we should learn to endure the gods— even Saturn, he said. He accepted that they all could bestow certain positive qualities. He believed that the more we understood and endured the planetary influences, the more the world opened to us. Everything was seen as having a lager meaning, a reason and place. Ficino's influence on Renaissance culture was profound. It was with the help of men like him that we started to leave behind the Dark Ages and Medieval customs.

---

[5] Reprinted by Spring Publications, University of Dallas, 1980.
[6] Between 1459 and 1477, Ficino translated the complete works of Plato, and thus was the first man for many centuries to rediscover him. See Vincent Cronin, *The Florentine Renaissance* (London: Pimlico, 1992), p. 130.

However, the adverse side of the intellectual genius of the time can be seen in Niccolo Machiavelli: he became secretary to the new Florentine Republic, declared a year after Lorenzo de' Medici's death. A brilliant political philosopher and cynical statesman, he is still notorious after five hundred years for his book on statecraft, *The Prince*, in which he advocated an amoral and opportunistic manipulation of people as the ideal way to advance the interests of both state and self.[7]

We have seen a great many changes, both positive and negative, during the 20th century. With the configuration of Saturn, Uranus, and Neptune (1988-1991) occurring again after five hundred years—but this time in the sign of Capricorn—we might expect some great shift in the material, economical, and governmental policies of our world.

Many alterations have indeed been taking place in the material structure (Capricorn-Saturn) of the world, and world governments. Much of the framework of society seems now to be going through profound breakdowns, as old systems are seen for what they are. But if any society is to be reborn, this can only come about through each individual's acceptance of his or her own desire nature, including its shadow side.[8] A new world based on Neptune's and Uranus' higher attributes can never work in an active sense until this is achieved. Certainly the new age will not be without birth pangs for the individual and the species, for collectively it signifies the need for great changes to the physical and spiritual world as a whole.

In a painting by Johfra, the Dutch artist and philosopher, symbolizing the sign of Aquarius, he shows a distant mountain with a pathway leading to it passing through a gateway formed by a skull. This is the gateway of Capricorn—the sign ruled by Saturn. Once through the gateway (Saturn-Capricorn), we climb to the top of the mountain (Uranus-Aquarius) where we acquire more insight, and thus can never act or react in the same way again to our fellow man. From the height of this new consciousness, we may look down and see those in the valley below, for our heightened awareness brings to us the complete knowledge of our kinship with all our fellow beings. Now it seems we are beckoned on by a spirit imparting to us a new universal law and understanding.

---

[7] Niccolo Machiavelli. *The Prince*. Trans. G. Bull (London: Penguin Classics, 1970).

[8] See *The Saturn/Pluto Phenomenon*, pp. 38, 39.

Neptune, because of its character, has always been a vague influence, but more conscious integration is possible if we can understand better its role within ourselves. We hear that the new age is rapidly advancing, that humankind's consciousness is quickly expanding. Admittedly, nearly eighty years ago, writers like Alan Leo suggested that the majority of people were not yet evolved enough to understand the real role of Neptune. But now more and more individuals are rapidly advancing to a higher level of consciousness than ever before.

Trying to devise a way of working with Neptune was difficult when a traditional understanding of him was used, that is, as a symbolic Neptune figure. That is why I thought of balancing the material (Saturn) with the ideal (Neptune). This did bring in results which were certainly useful when working with Neptune placements. I have stressed before and repeat again that *Saturn is the basis for working with any planetary energy*: responsibility should be accepted for Saturn's placement before any real growth in self-awareness and transcendence can begin.

As the higher Saturn energy is "true strength and unity with the self," so the highest interpretation of the Neptune energy seems to be "divine love free from illusions." The Neptune Meditation (see page 61) therefore should be used in conjunction with the Saturn Meditation (page 71).

Neptune may induce too much negative idealization of any cause, thus defeating the very object it seeks to achieve. This can occur on many levels, including the more personal one. Those particularly interested in humanitarian causes often have a strongly placed Neptune, but when such people's ideals become distorted—due to other personality defects—they cannot ever obtain their perfected and desired result. While it is desirable to stop the suffering of our fellow beings, for instance, this can only be achieved when the consciousness of each individual is lifted. The same rule applies to everything, including those in control of, and those opposed to, the governments of the day. We must develop a more conscious acknowledgment of our ideals and learn to recognize the evasions which are caused by our own character when we are dealing with any relevant idealistic issue.

If Neptune can cause false and escapist ideals to be generated, Uranus—when improperly used—causes breakdown, revolution and catastrophe. Many have embraced the ideals of Uranus in the name of humanity, and many bloody revolutions have been fought in the search for a more equal society, but often negative and destructive tendencies have predominated, because of humankind's unevolved nature on other levels. Uranus can cause erratic and antisocial behavior in its more unconventional and harmful mode. Revolution and eccentric behavior patterns fall under this influence. On a personal level, people with a strongly-placed Uranus seem to be "different" in some way. Whether this quality of being different produces positive or negative results will depend on other factors. There is nearly always a strong self-will and a certain amount of tension present with this planet prominent.

If we look to the discovery of Uranus in 1781, we see it heralds a time of revolt through bloody war and turmoil; it also heralds the beginning of the industrial revolution. If we then view the change in humankind's working conditions after the start of industry, we certainly see that, although it was progressive to the world in one sense, it also enslaved a great many workers to a life of bondage and drudgery within the factories and mills. Look at uprisings and the overthrowing of governments, at national rebellions, at France and Russia after their great revolts, and you see no great and universal scheme replacing the old order, but just more enslavement for most of the masses.

Equally, however, we should recognize that, by trying to hold on to old, outmoded systems of behavior—either personally or collectively—we may suffer considerably through that element in Uranus which requires change. Yet, on the other hand, if we should prematurely tear down any structure that seems to impede our growth, we may cause irreparable damage to an area that only requires a changed consciousness. So, how do we deal with this most unusual influence? For, when Uranus signifies the need for change, then a less orthodox and more universal approach is required in some area.

Uranus signifies the unconventional and unusual. If you accept that Uranus will show you a "new" version of reality quite different from that which you have previously experienced, you then begin to understand that this new reality (actuality) can only live and grow when grounded in the world. Here again we have to look to the structure of Saturn before we can successfully deal with Uranus for, when Saturn's natal placement is truly understood and worked with, we often find that Uranus allows us to begin to experience a new consciousness. We can discover a new way to work with old problems through recognizing where our unique talents may be found.

Uranus at best is the "Great Awakener" who will bring in a consciousness beyond ordinary understanding. For this to be grounded and used within human life requires that Saturn's lessons be recognized, for no true progress can be made into transcendental realms without Saturn.

When trying to find some image as a meditation symbol for Uranus, none could be found. When I surrounded myself and others with the imagery of this planet, no connective symbol seemed to present itself. Then, in a way typical of Uranus's nature, the answer came in a sudden revelation: there was no archetypal image really connected to this god, for was he not himself "Universal Thought," the "creative mind of God," the one who actually gave to humankind the ability to connect the other archetypal images to each other?

Thus in its highest order Uranus signifies the creative will or the creative power of the universal spirit. For this to be understood requires perhaps an intuition that can only be found through the effects of the transpersonal planets, as it is not based on any intellectual concepts that may derive solely from Mercury. Uranus in its purest form is the Higher Mercury, as Neptune is the Higher Venus. We can learn how to find our own way back from whence we came, but only after we have learned to direct our free will beyond the personal ego with its unconscious and often conflicting desires.

# 2

# NEPTUNE IN
# MYTHOLOGY, MUSIC, AND POETRY

> I begin to sing about Poseidon, the great god, mover of the earth and fruitless sea, god of the deep who is also lord of helicon and wide Aegae.
>
> —Homer[1]

It was possibly during the third century B.C. that the Neptune of the Romans took on the attributes of a much greater god called Poseidon and inherited his vast empire of the seas and rivers. This was about the time of the Roman invasion of Greece. In Greece there were many temples and statues to Poseidon; the temples were often built overlooking the sea, his special domain. Poseidon was a grandson of Uranus, a son of Cronos (Saturn), and brother of Zeus (Jupiter), and Hades (Pluto). Poseidon's rule was vast and he held sway over all the seas, rivers, and oceans. Homer gave him the title Enosichthon (meaning "earth-shaker") because he was the god of earthquakes. Perhaps it is a very significant title, for, as earth is sustained by water, he could shake it at will: thus land as well as sea were under the undulating influence of this deity.

In Homer's *Iliad* (Book XX), Poseidon's sister Hera, asked for his help in battle, but he replied: "Hera you must control yourself and not be so outrageously aggressive."[2] Later, when he was watching Achilles and Aeneas fighting, he turned to the other gods in concern, for Aeneas was no match for Achilles. Hera said he must decide for himself whether to rescue

---

[1] Homer, *The Iliad*, trans. E. U. Rieu (London: Penguin Books, 1964) pp. 68, 72.

[2] Homer, *The Iliad*, pp. 369, 374.

Aeneas or leave him alone. Poseidon decided to help and made for the place where Aeneas was engaged in battle. There he spread a mist before Achilles' eyes and swept Aeneas off the ground, placing him down on the edge of the battlefield where he would be safe.

Poseidon was Zeus' younger brother and equal by birth, but at times he complained of his brother's greater power, although no one ever quarreled about his own rule over the seas. Poseidon's need for possessions often brought about conflict with other gods, and his love affairs were too numerous to mention. His offspring, which were also legion, included Euphemus, Evadne, Cycnus and many others, as well as more malignant and monstrous beings: these last may have been symbolic of the terror primitive men must have felt for the ferocious storms at sea that could so easily destroy their ships. Another attribute of Poseidon was his ability to disguise himself while in pursuit of his many loves. He often took on the form of an animal in order to seduce the object of his lust. He became a dolphin to woo his wife, Amphitrite (the female personification of the sea, and a daughter of Oceanus) a stallion to ravish Demeter (Ceres), and Medusa; and a ram to beguile Theophane. There is, however, also a much deeper meaning behind all of these stories, for the stories of Poseidon were in some ways a mythical narration connected to the flooding and destruction of Atlantis.[3]

If we look at the god Poseidon as the deity from whom Neptune took rule, we find that in ancient mythology he was also symbolically acknowledged as the savior, or the higher part of humanity that wakes up the emotional nature and safely guides it—in other words, the part that presides over the soul. This same god in Indian mythology is known as Vishnu, and to the classical writers of India he also was the savior, and god of tender devotion and love. Vishnu descended to Earth in various world cycles to save mankind. He is depicted seated on a white lotus flower, and by him his most beautiful and talented wife Lakshmi, who was symbolic of creative energy; she who was born from the churning of the sea. The word *vish* means "to pervade," and so Vishnu is known as that presence which per-

---

[3] See Madame Blavatsky, *The Secret Doctrine*, Vol. 2 (London: Theosophical Publishing House, 1893), pp. 765, 766. This book has been reissued many times in the United States and in England.

vades everything; he is a Hindu deity of the greatest importance. There are many myths connected to Vishnu where he dons a disguise to achieve his chosen goal—much like Poseidon—but in the case of Vishnu it is usually to save humankind, and on such occasions he incarnates in an avatar[4] in human or sometimes animal form. Vishnu is also associated with the primordial waters as Narayana. In myth, Krishna was merged with Vishnu and was known as the preserver. Vishnu also took on the form of Shiva in his role as dissolver. Many regard Vishnu as the supreme creator, and it is said that from him came Brahma.

In myth and legend, stories abound with strong Neptunian influences. In Homer's *Odyssey* there is the story of how Odysseus blinded the cyclops Polyphemus, a son of Poseidon, and through this suffered Poseidon's lifelong enmity, having to resist spells and overcome monsters and other evils. In one instance, he stopped his crew's ears up with wax and had himself tied to the ship's mast so that none of the ship's company would succumb to the alluring voices of the Sirens summoned by Poseidon to destroy them, for their beguiling song would enslave whoever heard its seductive melody, and their ship would have been wrecked on the Sirens' island and they themselves destroyed.

There are also many stories about the Land of the Faeries, a land that seldom released those who wandered into it—a severe warning to those who were unaware of the dangers that lay in the depths of the unconscious. Even Merlin, the archetypal wizard of Arthurian legend, was trapped forever in an enchanted wood, betrayed by his love for Nineve, whom he had entrusted with some of his magic art: this legend fully expresses the overwhelming power of the unconscious forces of the psyche, as symbolized by Neptune.

Art, music, and poetry are often formed by strongly Neptunian influences, influences that have to find expression beyond the ordinary intellect. Musically, Neptune is connected to most stringed instruments, such as the violin, viola, harp and cello, for as the vibrations of an earthquake run through the veins of the earth, so do the vibrations of Neptune run through our own bodies. Whether we are able to channel them in their sublimity or

---

[4] Avatar; the descent of a Hindu deity to earth in a visible form—the ten Avatars of Vishnu are the best known.

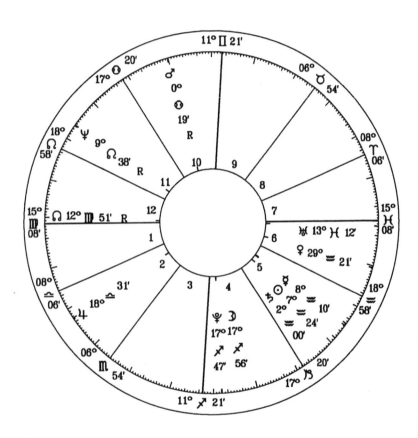

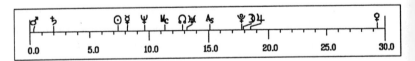

*Chart 2. Mozart's chart. January 27, 1756, 8:00 P.M. GMT. Placidus houses. Data from* The Blackwell Data Collection, *published by Astrolabe. Chart calculated by Astrolabe using* Nova Printwheels.

not remains to be seen. Mozart, although an extreme and unusual example of musical genius, experienced a great many physical and mental problems within his daily life, his 5th house Sun conjuncts Saturn and Mercury in Aquarius all in opposition to Neptune in Leo in the 11th house. See Chart 2 on page 14. He was, however, a channel for the most exquisite musical inspiration.

Many great poets, including Coleridge, Wordsworth, Shelley, and Keats had Neptune strongly placed. Usually if Neptune is strong by placement and aspect within the chart, a certain difficulty with the material world seems inevitable, with the result—in Coleridge's case—that he became addicted to opiates. It is almost as if by tasting the divine source it becomes difficult to live without it, so addiction to drugs or alcohol and other forms of escapism are common, and more so with the hard aspects. See Chart 3 on page 16. In one poem by Coleridge called "Dejection," he speaks of how his soul talks to him through his imagination and combats the pain of human life: he had Venus conjunct Saturn and Neptune in the 9th house.

> And from the soul itself must there be sent
> A sweet and potent voice, of its own birth,
> Of all sweet sounds the life and element!
>
> O pure of heart! thou need'st not ask of me
> What this strong music in the soul may be![5]

The Ocean, which is Neptune's domain, has always been symbolic of the great unconscious, and trial by water would adequately describe the more challenging aspects to this planet. As water will wear away a stone, so this influence will wear away at us, until we begin to recognize its sacred source. Certain initiates of old would be buried alive for three days in order to contact this divine soul principle within the unconscious, then on the third day be reunited with life. A similar initiation in varying degrees and stages was common to many different cultures: the unconscious has always been the birthright of humankind, the Soul the source of all

---

[5] Samuel Taylor Coleridge, "Dejection," IV, l. 10-12; V, l. 1, 2. *The Penguin Book of Religious Verse* (London: Penguin, 1963), p. 67.

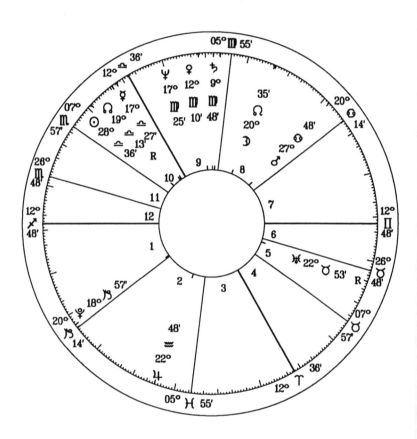

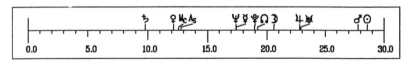

*Chart 3. Coleridge's solar chart. October 21, 1772. Placidus houses. Data from* The Blackwell Data Collection, *published by Astrolabe. Chart calculated by Astrolabe using* Nova Printwheels.

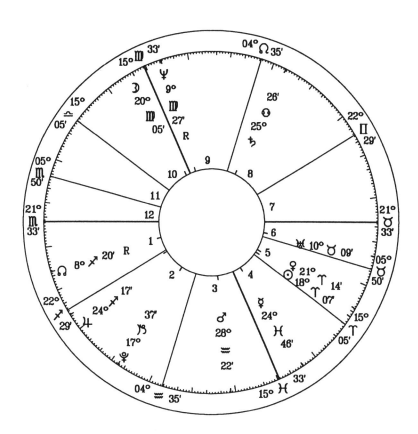

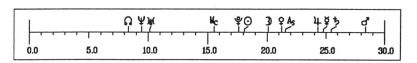

Chart 4. Wordsworth's chart. April 7, 1770, 10:00 P.M. GMT. Placidus houses. Data from The Blackwell Data Collection, published by Astrolabe. Chart calculated by Astrolabe using Nova Printwheels.

inspiration. The Soul also speaks to us through beauty and often we find this beauty in nature. Wordsworth, whose chart shows Neptune in Virgo in the 9th house trine Uranus in Taurus in the 6th house, addresses this often in his poetry. See Chart 4 on page 17.

> . . . And I have felt
> A presence that disturbs me with the joy
> Of elevated thoughts; a sense sublime
> Of something far more deeply interfused,
> Whose dwelling is the light of setting suns,
> And the round ocean and the living air,
> And the blue sky, and in the mind of man;
> A motion and a spirit, that impels
> All thinking things, all objects of all thought,
> And rolls through all things.[6]

[6] William Wordsworth, "Lines composed a few miles above Tintern Abbey," lines 93-102. *Six Centuries of Great Poetry* (New York: Dell Publishing, 1955), pp. 335, 336.

# 3

# NEPTUNE IN
# SIGN AND HOUSE

> Neptune represents that part of us which yearns, in the heart of our being, to dissolve those boundaries and divisions that prevent us experiencing our essential oneness with the rest of life.
>
> —Howard Sasportas[1]

Neptune is the eighth planet in our solar system, and orbits the Sun every 164.8 years, spending an average period of just under fourteen years in each sign. It is a giant gas (hydrogen, helium, methane) planet, its light so dim it cannot be seen with the unaided eye. Neptune is believed to have a hard rocky core covered by ice. The camera of the Voyager space probes, which passed Neptune in August 1989, revealed a wide variety of cloud features. Neptune has two named moons (Nereid and Triton) and six more as yet unnamed moons, discovered by Voyager 2 probes.[2] Some astronomers have even suggested that Pluto (the ninth and outer planet of our solar system) was a former Moon of Neptune's that escaped.

As Neptune stays in one sign for several years, it must be regarded as a planet that affects generations. However, Neptune's influence should be read in conjunction with Pluto's (see *The Saturn/Pluto Phenomenon*, pp. 121-134), since both planets will have effect on whole generations and events as they transit each sign.

---

[1] Howard Sasportas, *The Gods of Change* (London: Arkana, 1989), p. 116.

[2] Voyager, two U.S. space probes, originally Mariners. Voyager 1, launched September 1977, passed Jupiter March 1979, and reached Saturn November 1980. Voyager 2 was launched August 1977 on a slower trajectory that took it past Jupiter July 1979, Saturn August 1981, Uranus January 1986, and Neptune August 1989.

Due to Pluto having a very strongly elliptical orbit, it is on occasion actually closer to the Sun than Neptune: this is so between 1979 and 1999. During the middle and all through the second half of the 20th century, Neptune and Pluto are spending approximately the same number of years in each constellation (roughly fourteen) although Pluto can spend up to thirty-six years in a sign. Neptune's transit through Libra (1942-1943 to 1955, 1956, 1957) brought in an idealistic, sometimes deluded view of relationships, while Pluto's transit through Leo (1939 to 1958) engendered a very individualistic generation, particularly in regard to self-awareness, love, and relationships (the generation that believed in flower power and followed hippy cultures).

The following generation had Neptune in Scorpio (1955, 1956, 1957, to 1970) and Pluto in Virgo (1956, 1957, 1958, to 1971, 1972) and they, as teenagers, seemed fascinated by the seamier side of life, as shown by their taste for punk and punk music. They became increasingly angry when systems that had supported their parents were washed away, transformed or changed (Uranus was also in Virgo 1961-1962 to 1969), culminating in a general lack of employment caused by industrial rearrangement and deterioration of standards. Many of this generation—now in their late 20s and 30s—are primarily responsible for the attitudes expressed in the media, and the general focus of life in the 1990s!

Consider Neptune's transit through Capricorn 1984-1998, remembering also the effect of Uranus and Saturn[3] and Pluto's transit through Scorpio 1984-1995, and you see how each planetary influence affects us, and is translated into the tremendous upheavals predicted for this period in history, as we quickly approach the millennium. Neptune and Pluto will continue to spend approximately the same number of years in each sign until Pluto's orbit around the Sun starts to accelerate in the early part of the 21st century.

Neptune's placement in our charts shows us where we tend to be idealistic and escapist. Once these areas are brought into focus, more conscious integration of the Neptunian influence is possible. The chart often needs to be read in its entirety—with particular attention to Saturn's placement—before Neptune's role can be seen with any clarity.

The following section explains the probable effects of Neptune's placement in sign and house: the sign Neptune falls in will be common to

---

[3] See Introduction and chapter 1.

your particular generation, while the house will show the more personal effects of Neptune in your chart. Aspects to Neptune should also be noted, particularly aspects to the Sun, Moon, Mercury, or Ascendant. The house Neptune rules or co-rules is also significant, though to a much lesser degree.

The effect of Neptune will be to unfocus and spiritualize the area of the chart where it is placed, and this will also apply to the planets which Neptune aspects.

## NEPTUNE IN THE 1ST HOUSE
**(In Aries, influencing the generation born 2026 to 2039)**

The 1st house is the house of personality, the lens of the camera through which you project your *persona* to the world. Neptune in the 1st house therefore unfocuses the image of yourself that you project, and you will never be quite sure how others perceive you. Neptune in the 1st house bestows upon you great sensitivity of feeling and, however you may represent yourself outwardly, you usually end up feeling uncomfortable with forceful individuals.

This position gives you a very idealistic nature, but the nature of your idealism will be determined by other areas of your chart. For instance, the ideals generated by a person seeking answers to the mysteries of life may be very different from those of a person engaged in artistic endeavors within the fashion industry—although they may well co-exist. Usually you are very helpful to others, even to the point of great self-sacrifice. However, unscrupulous people will often take advantage of your kind nature and "use" you; this is partly because you have difficulty in forming a true sense of your own identity, and reflect what you think others *want* to see in you, rather than showing them your own unique individuality.

If there are difficult aspects to Neptune in a chart, delusion and escapist tendencies will be common. There may be an inner need to sacrifice yourself to a cause which, in some cases, may be escapist in the extreme. Usually you will use your personality in an unegoistic way, such as in serving others, often without payment or reward. Should the aspects to Neptune be flowing, there will still be sacrifice, but it will have a more positive outcome, as for instance when a person is devoted to a humanitarian cause, or becomes a channel for creative images to flow through, expressing inspiration in music, art, or literature for the enjoyment and inspiration of others.

The difference between the positive and negative aspects is that the negative ones usually carry with them a lot of deluded and escapist principles, which in the long term cause a great deal of unhappiness. Depression is common with the difficult aspects; so is escape through drink or drugs, and indulgence in other forms of escapism.

Look to Saturn first, and find out what this influence implies, before trying to understand just how Neptune affects your life. Start to recognize—as well as to put into practice in a realistic way—your own needs within all relationships, including those with your family, with your partner, and within society as a whole. This may be hard to do, and you will often struggle to achieve clarity or thought in these areas, but it is necessary that you become more singular and individualistic, in order to bring your compassionate personality into clearer focus to benefit both yourself and others, as well as the world as a whole.

## NEPTUNE IN THE 2ND HOUSE
### (In Taurus, influencing the generation born 2039 to 2052)

The 2nd house is associated with your inner values and resources, the money you earn, as well as your possessions—and remember that possessions can cover a wide field. Neptune in the 2nd house will therefore unfocus, and spiritualize around, the above issues.

You can be vague and confused when it comes to the money you earn and your material possessions, as well as your considerable talents and resources which, while often unrecognized by you, may be recognized and exploited by others. If running your own business, you should seek the help of an honest accountant—I say *should*, for often the people you trust with your money can be quite elusive, not to say devious at times. In business or not, you may at times get into quite difficult and confusing situations where finances are involved. You may also spend a lot of time daydreaming about all the things you would buy if only you had the means. Sometimes if may be difficult for you to see any boundary between your possessions and those of others, therefore the more negative aspects could cause you to live by relying on the generosity of others.

The more positive aspects imply that you are a very generous and giving individual, one who would often prefer to give to others rather than yourself. Again, the difference between the positive and negative aspects is that the former carry far less delusion, and thus allow a more considered approach to giving.

For a better understanding of Neptune in the 2nd house, first trace Saturn's implications within your life's structure: this will help you to see why you have a need for false values. Then look at all the value systems that influence your life. Do you appreciate your gifts, talents, and personal qualities? Do you make the best use of them? Or do you just seek self-worth through what you can possess and own, and/or through how others value you? By understanding your real values, you grow fair and just, and it is likely you will develop a deep, positive and rewarding appreciation of music and the arts. Your doubts about developing your own innate talents and abilities will lessen as you learn to use them for your own benefit: in so doing, you will add to your own value system, while at the same time you give more beauty and meaning to other people's lives.

# NEPTUNE IN THE 3RD HOUSE
## (In Gemini, influencing the generation born 2052 to 2066)

As this position is connected to mental ability, speech and communication may often be difficult and confused; although your thoughts are often hard to define, images usually come easily. You are likely to love music and poetry. You are a dreamer, fervently wishing to be able to communicate your thoughts to others, but often finding this almost impossible, for the right words seem so difficult for you to find.

Another difficulty with Neptune in the 3rd house—especially with the harder aspects—is that you may sometimes have difficulty in being truthful; indeed, you may not even be sure what the truth is. Try to be scrupulously honest, for it is so easy for you to slip into half-truths and make-believe. You easily pick up subtle variations around you, feeling that you almost know what others are thinking. Sometimes your intuition is amazingly accurate, at other times, however, something you feel quite certain about may actually be nothing more than a figment of your own wishful thinking and/or your unconscious fears.

Look to Saturn's position in your chart to identify why you are prone to wishful thinking, and to identify some of your fears and the causes of your despondency. Working with Saturn will help to develop rational and realistic thought patterns as well as the more intuitive ones. Decisions then become easier to make, and creative inspiration often flows. Try to use Neptune's higher attributes in the application of some high ideal or spiritual aspiration. Meditation is often a good way to start.

## NEPTUNE IN THE 4TH HOUSE
**(In Cancer, influencing the generation born 1902 to 1916)**

The 4th house represents home and family, mother or mother figures[4] in your life. It also embodies emotional reactions, many of which are habitual and are the result of early childhood experiences. With Neptune in the 4th house, there will be vague longings connected to an image within your psyche of the perfect home and/or emotional relationship. Deep down you may find it hard to be emotionally independent, always yearning back to the past.

With difficult aspects, transits, or progressions to Neptune in the 4th house, you may constantly seek the ideal home environment—though often you end up disappointed and disheartened. Great sacrifice and dissatisfaction may be experienced within the home as well as within the family group. Your mother's influence may likewise be vague and ill-defined, or she herself may be of an evasive type. Sometimes you yearn for the good old days, remembering everything through a rosy haze, even trying to re-create your childhood environment in some way. You may sacrifice yourself considerably in order to bring this re-creation about.

With Neptune positively placed in the 4th house, your domestic environment may be a place of great perfection and beauty, or a haven for yourself and others away from the harsh realities of the world. You may surround yourself with beautiful belongings which you share with others in some way. Your mother may be a figure whom you revere, or the person you try to emulate in some way.

---

[4] This may on occasion be the father, if he took on the more caring and nurturing role, as symbolized by the 4th house and Cancer.

In order to better focus Neptune's influence in the 4th house, first look to Saturn and those implications within your chart. Define why there is a need for escapism within the home or in your emotional life—for even with the good aspects to Neptune escapism will be strong. Uncertain and confusing conditions could undermine your home and/or family relationships because of past dreams centering around perfection in these areas.

Once Saturn's message is realized, you will gain clearer insight into all home, family and emotional needs and be able to put them into context. You learn that true stability and security are only to be found within yourself, and with this realization comes great emotional insight into your own "real" and lasting needs, wherever your home may be.

# NEPTUNE IN THE 5TH HOUSE
## (In Leo, influencing the generation born 1916 to 1929)

The 5th house is the house of love, love affairs, affection, of enjoyment and pleasure; it is the house of the Self and of creative expression, also the house of children as our created offspring. It is in these areas that Neptune's influence will be brought to bear. With this placement, your romantic inclinations are likely to be strong, but vague and confused situations often arise through unrealistic attitudes and utopian expectations in connection with love and romance. Initially, your new love may be perceived through a gossamer haze of idealistic dreams, or, depending on other factors within the chart, you may never be satisfied for very long with any lover, and a new one will always come along to tempt you away. There is likely to be the one great love that you lost and cannot forget.

As the 5th house is the house of the Self, there may (depending on other planetary positions and aspects in the chart) be a deluded sense of self, with much self-aggrandizement, self-approbation and self-conceit: these are false expressions of an overdeveloped and unbalanced ego, and can only delude and generate more illusion until recognized as such.

As the 5th is the house of your created offspring, there may be idealism and often sacrifice in connection with your children. You may wish them to be perfect or exemplary in some way, or, in spite of their weaknesses you may see them as veritable angels. There may also be times when you end up disappointed and disenchanted by their manners and actions. Children can often take on a very idealized image for you with this position of Neptune, even if you have no offspring of your own.

Recognize Saturn's message within your chart before you try to understand how Neptune's ideals affect your life. Develop true humility and compassion, and nurture the freedom to be a child yourself. Let go of any false need for prestige or glamor in all creative endeavors, and instead allow Neptune's expressive inspiration to flow naturally. At some point in your life, you may experience a highly idealistic love, and, although some sacrifice or disappointment may well occur, the experience can be of great help to you in finding out who and what you really are.

## NEPTUNE IN THE 6TH HOUSE
### (In Virgo, influencing the generation born 1929 to 1943)

The 6th house is the house of work and service, of health and diet. There may be a great deal of sacrifice, as well as confusion and illusion centering around some or all of these areas. The work involved is not only your employment or trade, but also the duty and service you give to family, friends and associates. With the more difficult aspects, it is not uncommon for you to become a slave to work in some form, or to the collective needs of other people.

The body may not be robust, with illness often difficult to diagnose. The health can be impaired, often—although not always—by overwork. A variety of health problems predominate, and these are often of a vague and hard-to-define nature.[5]

Another manifestation of Neptune in the 6th house is that you are always seeking perfection, not uncommonly in connection with employment and service of all kinds. Others' lack in this area often causes you sadness and disillusionment, since you often feel forced to shoulder the burdens. The more positive aspects to Neptune help you find a vocation through which your visionary and compassionate qualities can be expressed in ways that serve the collective needs of others.

---

[5] The Flower and Gem Remedies may be particularly beneficial to you; see page 87.

By better understanding and working with Saturn's placement within your chart, you begin to realize why you have sought such perfection, as well as why you have felt the need to make so many sacrifices in your life. Aspects to Neptune will help you to identify more fully where the sacrifices have been made and the perfection sought. Once these are seen in a clearer context, you move on to serve others in a more universal way—free from guilt, servitude, and the unconscious influence of more personal emotional needs.

# NEPTUNE IN THE 7TH HOUSE
## (In Libra, influencing the generation born 1943 to 1957)

The 7th house is connected to relationships in general. It is the house of the partner, as well as the shadow[6] aspects of your personality. This can be a difficult placement for Neptune, as other people—particularly the partner—are often not seen clearly, and it is not uncommon to find you do not know certain aspects of your partner at all. In traditional astrology, the 7th house was known as the house of open enemies; it is therefore likely, with Neptune in the 7th, that you may experience underhanded dealings from others, as well as vague and confused interaction with other people at certain times in your life when there are difficult aspects, transits, or progressions. Sometimes it will seem that, however hard you try, other people will perceive your intentions differently from how you intend them.

However, in spite of these difficulties, you are usually loyal within your close relationships, as well as idealistic in your expectations of others. With the more difficult aspects, a certain mistrust can be felt toward some people.

As the 7th house will also reflect your partner's qualities, he or she may be of a Neptunian type: sensitive, artistic, aesthetic and refined; or, conversely, someone addicted to drink or drugs; a struggling writer, artist, or musician; a vague and evasive person; or someone combining a little of all these things at different times.

Although this position of Neptune does require some sacrifice, you should not allow yourself—or your partner—to make continual sacrifices

---

[6] See *The Saturn/Pluto Phenomenon*, pages 38–39.

or to play the martyr role. To avoid some of the negatives manifesting, try to face reality by looking at Saturn's placement within your chart, and work to understand why the need exists for the evasion, escapism, or martyrdom in your more personal relationships.


## NEPTUNE IN THE 8TH HOUSE
### (In Scorpio, influencing the generation born from 1957 to 1970)

The 8th house is associated with others' money and values, as well as resources shared with others—including sexual and emotional involvements. The 8th house is also the house of death and transformation, and of in-depth psychology. Positive aspects to Neptune in the 8th house can give you spiritual and mystical insights into the more hidden and secret realms of knowledge and experience. Death, darkness, and transformation, the occult,[7] arcane (secret), and esoteric, may contain a certain fascination for you. Sometimes you may even have an inner knowledge which tells you that there is no death anywhere in the universe, only transformation.

As the 8th house is connected to all resources shared with others, you may experience some vague and uncertain states in the areas connected to emotional and sexual involvement with others. Sex often has a great fascination for you, and you can have many fantasies in this area. The difficulty here is that the real thing rarely comes up to your expectation, so you may always be dreaming of someone else rather than the person you are with. Occasionally, the more negative aspects to Neptune may cause sex to exert a powerful and magnetic influence over your life; this could confuse and worry you, or even influence you to become involved in certain distorted sexual activities. At the other extreme, you may choose instead to be celibate and renounce all sexual involvement.

Making money can often be important to you, but you may find yourself in difficulty when it comes to the money you owe to others. You may also experience some confusion over inheritance, or tax liabilities—which you may try to ignore.

---

[7] Those things relating to supernatural influences and that which is beyond human understanding.

By working with and understanding the influence of Saturn in your chart, you can—if you choose—begin to build more personal integrity into all your dealings with others, for discrimination and honesty are essential in all areas connected to this position of Neptune.

# NEPTUNE IN THE 9TH HOUSE
## (In Sagittarius, influencing the generation born 1970 to 1984)

The 9th house is the house of "god," of higher learning and wisdom; it is also the house associated with travel—both mental and physical—and the house of law and of ethical and moral values. With the difficult aspects and/or transits, you may find some confusion occurring in connection with your attendance at college or university. For instance, there may be some disappointment connected to college or other places of higher learning; you could find your degree does not help or satisfy you in the long term; or that you have taken the wrong subject; or you may have to drop out through poor concentration, or because of other Neptunian influences resulting in problems with drink or drugs, for instance.

Your spiritual and philosophical concepts are usually conceived on an intuitive plane, and therefore sometimes hard to define. Visions and dreams often can be prophetic, but during your early years you may not have the confidence to trust your own spiritual insights—however strong—accepting the philosophical and spiritual teachings of others, rather than developing the natural wisdom within yourself.

Often you may follow others' teachings and, although an inner sense tells you they are not for you, you do not always have the courage to stand up and say so; however, confidence usually develops with age. There is the possibility that sometime during your life you will experience mystical states which lift you above the normal experiences of everyday life. If this is the case, they will often be the inspiration which keeps you going, particularly when life becomes heavy and harsh.

As the 9th house is also the house of moral values, your morals may be high, although confusion and martyr-like experiences may evolve around some of your thoughts in these areas. Guilt can often undermine your deeper convictions, as can awareness of moral lapses in others. The more you understand and develop Saturn's structure—including the restrictions—within your life, the more you will trust that inner voice and your own special wisdom.

# NEPTUNE IN THE 10TH HOUSE
**(In Capricorn, influencing the generation born 1984 to 1998)**

Neptune in the 10th house will spiritualize, idealize, unfocus and sometimes delude your view of your position and ambitions in the world—including those connected to your career as well as your place in society. It will also have the same influence on anyone who wields authority over you, including your parents. Traditionally, this house represents the father.

Since Neptune can symbolize illusion, as well as delusion, you may have a romantic ideal connected to getting on in the world, or a vision of the perfect and ideal career. Sometimes this may be the dream that you work steadily toward, but it may be the dream that is never realized that leads to all kinds of disappointment. Try to learn to be more impersonal and look at your place within the world honestly and realistically; look also at any ideals you have which center around the "perfect career."

This position of Neptune can give an aesthetic appreciation of architecture (particularly stonework). Some with Neptune in the 10th house may have careers connected to buildings; or an idealistic career involving authority and the law; or work with governmental authorities which help to alleviate drug, alcohol, or other Neptunian dependencies. The career may also encompass any area involved with the uplifting of world consciousness, as seen in world wide campaigns to alleviate suffering, or those connected to world ecology. Sometimes you may produce the dreams and illusions of Neptune within the world (10th house), so that the career may be connected with the stage, or some other related field of entertainment.

With Neptune in the 10th house, you may experience an inbuilt shyness and sensitivity when in public or social situations, and you may therefore find it benefits you not to identify too much with social status or position. However, as Neptune is involved, you may not even be aware that you do! Saturn rules the 10th house, so look with particular interest to the whole of Saturn's structure within your life: this helps you to put some of Neptune's more positive but unrealized influence and potential in clearer focus.

# NEPTUNE IN THE 11TH HOUSE
**(In Aquarius, influencing the generation born 1998 to 2012)**

The 11th house is traditionally associated with friends, groups, and associations, as well as dreams and aspirations, therefore Neptune in this house will often spiritualize, unfocus, idealize as well as delude in these areas.

It is almost certain you will want to feel needed by your friends, as well as experiencing deep meaning through them. In matters connected to friendships and group activity you are likely to be altruistic, sensitive, and idealistic. Often you bring an idealism and inspiration into all friendships and group activities, as well as a compassion and kindness that uplifts other's consciousness as well as your own. The friends you feel the most comfortable with are likely to be those who are equally as sensitive and idealistic as yourself.

However, sometimes your excessive idealism may cause you to have unrealistic expectations of certain friendships, with the consequence of sometimes feeling "let down." The more difficult aspects and transits to Neptune can even produce unfounded fears and over-sensitivity, causing feelings of persecution within the group situation. If this is the case, try to balance your fears by bringing them all down to realistic levels of understanding in acknowledging Saturn's influence within your chart. By doing this, you start to take on more responsibility for yourself and your reactions within all friendships and group activities.

The more difficult aspects and transits to Neptune may cause you sometimes to come into contact with certain friends or groups who try to escape dealing with reality in a rather negative way, possibly through drink, drugs, or some other type of escapism, such as is found within the practices of certain "so-called" spiritual or religious groups. Again, by truly acknowledging Saturn's influence within your life, your visionary and altruistic attitude within all group activities can really help others to turn their idealistic dreams into a more focused and creative actuality.

# NEPTUNE IN THE 12TH HOUSE
**(In Pisces, influencing the generation born 2012 to 2026)**

The 12th house is associated with sacrifice, suffering, and confinement. It is also the house associated with the unconscious mind. Neptune, the planet of altruism and refined love, is the ruler of Pisces and the 12th house and therefore at home in this position.

You will make a great many sacrifices during your lifetime, and often your inner strength will be a source of great comfort both to yourself and others. However, at other times when you experience difficult transits or progressions to Neptune, your great sensitivity causes you periods of confinement, often with much sadness, depression, and guilt, as well as fears and doubt about the future. Through experiencing the disintegration of attachments and activities, you may suffer some inner instability, but also through this you begin to learn great tolerance for the weaknesses of others.

This position of Neptune can give a certain psychic sensitivity, but for this to be a positive influence, Saturn's role within your life should be fully developed and understood. Psychic influence can be very positive and connect you to a greater whole, but it can also disintegrate and destroy an unbalanced or undeveloped personality. By working to integrate the influence of Saturn within your life, you may sometimes *choose* to go into solitude, which brings to you an even better understanding of your greater spiritual identity, as well as of your place within the universe as a whole.

# 4

# NEPTUNE

> Neptune indicates a yearning to experience a state of oneness with all of life, a merger with the whole of existence, and the dissolution of all boundaries, feelings of separateness, and egocentricity.
>
> —Stephen Arroyo[1]

Neptune, planet of divine and universal love, idealism, and compassion is also the planet of delusion, false glamor, and escapism. How then are we affected by this planet in daily life? For it is true we all need an ideal to follow—and Neptune will often supply it. We must not forget that the Neptunian vision is intangible and unformed, and is very difficult to ground in the realms of practical realization or capability. Because of this, there is often a great disappointment when we actually experience the physical manifestation of the Neptunian dream. Confusion comes about because most people look for their fulfillment and full experience of spiritual ideals within material existence.

Difficult aspects between Neptune and personal planets usually indicate the need for spiritual growth in some specific area. This growth may come about through disillusionment, confusion, and complications, often linked with feelings of hopelessness. How the person reacts to this will be shown by the rest of the chart.

The greatest danger attached to Neptune seems to be in the outer glamor and delusion that this planet sometimes generates. Delusion is a deviation of the lower mind and stops logical patterns of thought; signifi-

---

[1] Stephen Arroyo, *Astrology, Karma & Transformation* (Sebastapol, CA: CRCS Publications, 1978), p. 125.

cantly, though, it turns up just as often in the chart of the highly intellectual person as in any other type of chart.

Neptune causes us to follow a dream or an ideal, but over-idealization can bring about much sadness, until we really understand what Neptune's role is. The Neptunian "ideal" is an attribute of the soul, and, if we try to ground this ideal completely in material life, we are bound to be disappointed, for matter (the material) cannot ever supply what we seek; the result will be dissatisfaction and disenchantment occurring somewhere within our life.

So how do we deal with this vague and often confusing longing within the soul? First it is essential to formulate and bring clearly into consciousness just what one's ideals and dreams are. This will take much time and thought, and needs to be done in as methodical a way as possible, because the information is so often hazy and unclear. Writing all information down, and then going through it again and again at a later date seems the best way. Until the ideal is brought into more tangible consciousness it cannot be fully understood, but remains a vague subliminal influence, which can in some cases be detrimental to peace of mind, and may obscure our own unique purpose on Earth.

The tarot card associated with Neptune is The Hanged Man—it is symbolic of the Higher Mind's descent and surrender to matter. The older tarot card versions of the Hanged Man show Prometheus—symbolizing the highest element in the human being—who takes on a voluntary sacrifice for the greater good. He hangs by one foot which is tied to a pole resting between two lopped trees—six branches having been cut off each—and every day he is constantly tortured. Will all his sacrifice and surrender come to nothing? He does not know, and can only wait, but he waits patiently, and in time the gods reward him for his submission, and he is given eternal life in spirit. If we recognize that this sacrifice is connected theoretically with the Christ's, and that the highest recognition of this energy within ourselves is to learn to love, we see just what the message of Prometheus—and in turn Neptune's—is.

Because of this, many people with the hard aspects from Neptune to personal planets will follow some path of self-renunciation. Many will experience difficulties in relationships and religion, as they subconsciously search for the sublime. Others will suffer martyr-like tendencies, and feel very misunderstood. The hard aspects will indicate self-deception in some form.

In fact, we can define Neptune's challenging aspects as phases of life wherein we learn about spiritual values and realities in a subtle way by experiencing disillusionment to the full![2]

If we look at Chart 5 (page 36) with hard aspects from Neptune affecting the Sun and Mercury, we see the chart of a man who tried to run his own business. He was interested in psychic and spiritual matters and was extremely kind and caring.

Peter had been married for several years and was devoted to his wife, who had suffered a series of incapacitating illnesses throughout their married life; Peter very much took on the role of protector as far as she was concerned. His chart has Mercury in Pisces and Sun in Aries, both in the 1st house, opposing Neptune in Libra in the 7th, the Sun was in good aspect to Saturn and Uranus in Gemini in the 3rd house, and Pluto in Leo in the 6th. He was responsible, strong, and very intuitive and clear on some levels, anxious to learn, widely read and very humanitarian, helping others whenever he could.

The hard aspects from Neptune to Peter's Sun and Mercury were highlighted and brought to the fore when transiting Neptune was square both. It was at this time that he started a business enterprise—which was very idealistic and aimed mainly at helping others—funded from a substantial inheritance. Unfortunately it seemed doomed from the start, and although friends and relatives offered help in many ways, it gradually went downhill, and when all the money had been used up, debts began to mount and eventually he was declared bankrupt.

Neptune's influence seemed to cause complete oblivion to what was going on regarding the business, and a lack of commonsense in every endeavor connected to it. At least, this is what appears to be the case if we look at it one way. Or maybe Peter was in tune with his destiny and accepted it without bitterness or rancor? Or was it some of both?

In any event he, and his wife ended up bankrupt and homeless, but he was apparently undaunted by the experience, and continued to try to help other people whenever he could. Neptune's compassion and sensitivity were in no doubt, but was there a lack of balance somewhere? Many people in the helping professions have hard aspects from Neptune, particularly to the Sun and Mercury. It often seems very difficult for them to

---

[2] Stephen Arroyo, *Astrology, Karma & Transformation*, p. 125.

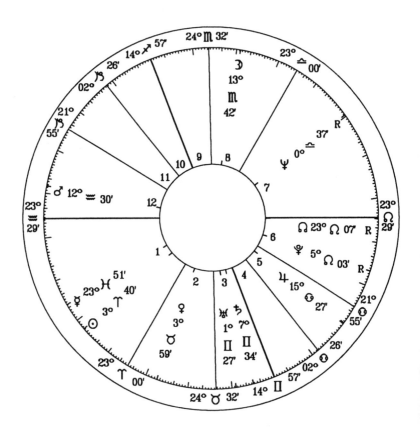

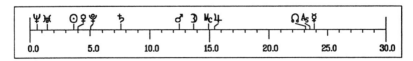

*Chart 5. Peter's chart. Birth data from family has been withheld for confidentiality. Placidus houses. Chart calculated by Astrolabe using* Nova Printwheels.

obtain a perspective on what is really going on in their life—but is this perhaps how it is meant to be?

Even the positive aspects from Neptune to personal planets cause any given actuality to be a subjective rather than an objective experience, for truth exists in many differing ways—and perhaps the only "real truth" can come from the Self, as Thoreau said.

> The only way to speak the truth is to speak lovingly; only the lover's words are heard. The intellect should never speak; it is not a natural sound.[3]

You may have noticed that all esoteric text, whether in the Bhagavad-Gita, Upanishads, *Pistis Sophia*,[4] or any other great teaching, have been written symbolically and can never be understood by the intellect alone. That is why many "clever" people have tried to decipher the text to little avail, and have only confused themselves and others still further by doing so. Each person who reads this sacred language takes from it only as much as his or her Higher Mind can understand, and no more; this is Universal Law. The Christ spoke and taught through parables, again so that each may find his or her own truth, for the fact is that the truth is different for each of us. To lie and deceive deliberately must, of course, be wrong, but truth in its purest form can only exist within the Soul. So by striving to live in the higher part of our natures, we must come nearer to that absolute reality of existence and understand more what Neptune's true message is.

> Hold fast to that which has neither substance nor existence.
> Listen only to the voice which is soundless.
> Look only on that which is invisible alike to the inner and outer sense.[5]

But if we are ever to start to do this, we must have first learned more about the lessons of Saturn; for we cannot ever lose ourselves before we have found ourselves, and in Saturn's message is found Neptune's illumination.

---

[3] Henry David Thoreau, *The Natural Man, A Thoreau Anthology, Journal*, March 15th, 1842, (Wheaton, IL: Theosophical Publishing House, 1978), p. 111.
[4] G. R. S. Mead, *Pistis Sophia* (New York: Spiritual Science Library, 1984).
[5] Mabel Collins, *Light on the Path* (Pasadena: Theosophical University Press, 1976), p. 15.

# 5

# NEPTUNE—
# CHAOS OR ECSTASY?

> The sea mirrors the sky above it; its waters rest upon the solid earth beneath. So does emotion bind thought to action and carry the fruits of action back again to the realms of thought; and it is through the gradual evolution of the emotional or psychic body that a man learns to choose aright his pleasures and his pains, and to look behind and beyond them for something that will outlast either.
>
> —Isabelle Pagan[1]

Neptune's depths lie in the formless ocean of Chaos, for Neptune represents the primordial ooze, or *prima materia*, the Great Mother, the essential element of all life as represented by Neptune's exaltation in Cancer. Neptune's influence is over all the astral realms, both higher and lower. Neptune is the planet that has little effect over the physical part of life, but is more a psychic or emotional influence.

There are many different regions which Neptune may hold sway over—from the height of compassion, idealism, inspiration, and vision, to the depths of escapism, deception, confusion, and fantasy. Within our life on Earth we may perceive many different and disparate levels of the Neptunian ideation. For instance, the poet Coleridge experienced tremendous inspiration and creativity, but also suffered the agony of the negative and escapist tendencies which could torture and incapacitate. (See Chart 3 on page 16.)

The imagination, which is so much part of the Neptune influence, can—in a chart with a strong Neptune involvement—cause both positive

---

[1] Isabelle M. Pagan, *From Pioneer to Poet* (London: Theosophical Publishing Society, 1911), p. 185. This book has been reissued by Theosophical Publishing House, London, 1978, as *Signs of the Zodiac Analyzed*.

and negative reactions. If we can begin to learn to use our imagination in a positive, creative sense, rather than in a negative or wishful-thinking sense, then the inner world becomes our oyster, and we do, indeed, find the pearl of great price.

When you read what follows, notice how you feel at the bottom of the castle, and how you feel as you go toward the light. Notice how many of the different scenes you can identify with, and remember that there are many diverse and sometimes similar chambers running off from the ones described. Bear in mind, too, that what is described is intended to be an archetypal vision, rather than a real scene from life.

• • •

There is a seashore swathed in a deep misty haze. A castle built of cloudy vapors rise from the fog swirling over the ocean, a castle of enormous structure, its foundations going right down into the depths of the waters. Its highest turrets reach up through the mists and haze into the sunlight hundreds and thousands of feet above. The castle has myriad rooms—both above and below the sea. There is a causeway leading to this watery palace, and a huge door which stands open. Inside there are misty steps leading downward to the base of the vast but ethereal edifice.

The bottom of the castle opens up into huge underwater caverns—there are many sea-monsters there, writhing in the murky gloom, monsters of nightmare and delirium, their swirling tentacles ready to wrap around the mind, creating fantastic fears and paranoid imaginings. This area then opens out into other vast caverns, gloomy and dark. There are figures here involved in all sorts of vicious, degenerate, and perverted acts. Their minds are warped and distorted: they seek sensation at its lowest level.

This dark and foggy cavern leads on into a similar area. Some of the people here are connected to the former place; there are figures lying on the floor, sad depraved figures, shadows of their true selves. These are minds that seek escape through addiction. Drugs, drink, and other evasions have enslaved both their senses and feelings. They grovel in the half-dark, hoping that this time they will find the escape they seek. A dark room opening from this chamber shows prisoners chained and held by their own minds, they weep and wail, plead and implore to be let free; but they are locked in their own wilderness, lost souls not able to recognize that which they seek.

An entrance along another dark and grim tunnel shows figures in sack-cloth and ashes, some doing penance on raw and bleeding knees, still others flagellating themselves. These are fanatics and false martyrs to many different causes—those who think that this is the way to find whatever god they seek. Up another gloomy corridor is a room with an open door. There are people sitting around a large table. It is some sort of seance. Strange and mischievous astral shapes lurk in the air above the group and the misguided onlookers think they are getting a message from on high.

There are many such corridors and rooms all around, and it seems difficult to find a way out of the darkness. Eventually a little more light appears. Looking inside the nearest door, you see what appear to be printing presses and men of intellect writing the news of the day. But what is this? Honesty does not exist here: the only important thing is sensationalism and misrepresentation to generate ever larger sales. The truth does not matter in this particular establishment, but has been sacrificed on the altar of greed.

There seem to be bright, glaring lights coming from a room nearby. Inside is the world of glamorous unreality—the false and meaningless are here, and shallowness of character masked by insincere flattery and empty gestures. Another room opening from this has much softer light, so as to disguise the huge web-like nets hanging all around. This is where the seducer and seduced are to be found. Temptation beckons from every strand in every web, and enticing music plays to lull the senses and ensnare the mind. The air is claustrophobic and it is good to get outside again. Can any way be found out of this lower-mind labyrinth?

After much searching down blind and murky passageways, witnessing various scenes of mayhem, confusion and chaos, the sound of laughter and children's voices are heard. It really is lighter here! This appears to be the place of happy memories, sunlit days, and pleasant outings. It brings warmth back into the limbs and some hope back to the heart. There is another room that opens off this; it is the room of happy dreams, where pleasant and delicious thoughts drift in and out of the air, swelling and withdrawing as the sea on the shore. It is a place of escape from the harshness of life, a gentle and safe abode, a haven to escape to for those who can find it. Many such chambers open from this one, there is a pleasant and languid feeling in the air, the corridors are sunny and peaceful—how different from the areas below.

The sound of beautiful music is heard. Through an open door are seen creative artists at work. There is the painter whose vision lifts his thoughts to higher realms where the creative elements then mix and blend on the virgin canvas. And here is the musician who becomes one with her composition, inseparable as the river that runs into the sea. And the poets holding the beauty of their thoughts within their minds then gently molding them into words with which to express their revelations to others.

Another passageway leads to an even more rarefied atmosphere. An air of wisdom permeates the place. Here is the true mystic, the person no longer enslaved by lower mind illusions, but developed in true compassion and understanding. This person seeks no glory, for there is none in the sense that most people know it. She or he lives in harmony with nature and seeks nothing more than human life's unfolding, realizing that life on Earth is no more than a learning process formed within a dream.

Now there is a great beauty and light all around, far removed from earthly suffering and sorrow. This is the place of perfect harmony. Dante walks with his Beatrice; here is found the mystical marriage of the alchemists, and the "Divine Union" of souls that is sought within all faithful lovers' hearts.

The light is now so pure that it can only be compared to the light of the spiritualized Sun. Here is a Paradise where wondrous gardens bloom and fountains glisten in rapturous joy, while paths lead down through sacred groves to rivers of delight. All around are heaven's hosts and love eternal; a landscape full of radiance and spreading luminosity, of lights and colors so wonderful to behold that words cannot ever match the splendor there, or describe the celestial radiance of this most glorious realm. We drift into heavenly rapture. But alas at last we wake—has it all been a dream—or is it life that is the dream?

• • •

Neptune's influence must of necessity cause us to seek some form of escape from the physical world; it remains to be seen whether this escape will allow the mind to soar, or pull it down into the deepest purgatory. All forms of escape from the physical are manifestations of the character and influence of Neptune, for it can seduce and ensnare, or uplift and inspire: we must learn to understand and work with Neptune more, if we are to identify this unique but well-hidden message.

# 6

# NEPTUNE AND LOVE

I seem to have loved you in numberless forms, numberless times,
In life after life, in age after age forever.
My spell-bound heart has made and re-made the necklace of songs
That you take as a gift, wear round your neck in your many forms
In life after life, in age after age forever.

—Rabindraneth Tagore[1]

The "ideal" that Tagore writes about is perhaps the basic conception within all love. This is the higher Neptunian vision, but for many—especially those with hard aspects from Neptune to Venus—it is a love often deluded, seldom happy, maybe fulfilled, but only for a short while.

Sometimes this love is projected onto a partner who is unavailable for some reason, and on occasion a figure not even met. It can be the love which searches through countless lifetimes for the complementary part of its soul in order to become whole, and this can cause both positive and negative reactions. Always this person is reaching for a love beyond himself or herself—for a sublime union. With the hard aspects it is almost as if he or she is forced to go down wrong alleys in order to bring forth new and universal understanding. Charles Carter describes the disharmonious aspects between Venus and Neptune as ". . . bestowing a divine discontent . . . and varying from a petulant or peevish attitude, to a noble aspiration and persistent endeavour to seek for a fuller realisation of inner vision."[2]

---

[1] Rabindraneth Tagore, "Unending Love," from *Selected Poems* (London: Penguin, Modern Classics, 1985), p. 49.
[2] Charles Carter, *The Astrological Aspects* (London: L. N. Fowler & Co., 1930), pp. 138, 139.

I remember a woman I met several years ago, who was, to all appearances, very normal and balanced. She was in her early 50s, had been married for well over twenty years, and had two grown children. She ran her own successful business, and life seemed quite good to her. But she had one great source of discontent: she could not be with the man she loved. The unusual story she told me was as follows, and I will leave readers to form their own conclusions. I cannot remember her whole chart, but do remember she had Venus conjunct Neptune.

The story she told was that one day while listening to the radio, she heard a man's voice that she recognized—how she knew it she could not explain. She tried to find out whose voice it was, but to no avail. A few months later, while watching television, she heard the same voice and this time she found out the actor's identity; the interesting part was, she was utterly convinced that this man was her soul mate. She lived and breathed just to think of the time she would be with him. A year or so later he was at a theater in her part of the country and she went to see him.

After that, wherever and whenever she could, she followed him around the different theaters where he was performing—and even managed to see him backstage on a couple of occasions. She never told him of her love, but her whole life was planned around him. It may seem silly, even laughable, but to her it was very real and, as she explained, he remained *her only reason for living*. We can think of many considerations why this should happen: for instance, she spoke of the fact that her marriage had never been happy, so was this some form of escape? Or could he really have been her soul mate? Perhaps there were other reasons. I suppose no one will ever really know; but this type of experience—though usually in a milder form—can be one of the effects of Venus and Neptune in difficult aspect.

Although not all hard aspects between Neptune and Venus will produce similar experiences, there always seems to be delusion concerned with a form of love, even if that *love* is for money or work. For instance, a woman having a Venus-Saturn conjunction in the 12th house opposite Neptune in the 6th, worked exceptionally hard and long hours with her partner to make money. This was very important to her, as it meant security for her family. They were giving an excellent service to the public but they often worked at the expense of her and her partner's health and peace of mind. Because Venus was also conjunct Saturn, I suppose it brought in the *added sacrifice made for duty*. Another chart having Venus in the 12th house opposite Neptune in the 6th, caused the person always to make great sacrifices to the current love, with the consequence of eventually being let down and suffering great disappointment and pain. He had Saturn and Mars in the 5th house which also must have affected his love-life. Another person with Venus in the 5th house opposite Neptune in the 11th had numerous love affairs with friends: she could not seem to differentiate between friendship and sexual relationships. She also had emotional problems which accentuated the circumstances.

Margaret Thatcher has Venus in the 1st house square a Moon-Neptune conjunction in Leo on the midheaven. See Chart 6 on page 46.

It is interesting when considering Venus-Neptune aspects to look also at the emotional conflicts that lie in other areas of the chart. As Venus is exalted in Cancer, and the Moon is the ruler of this sign, it seems necessary to trace the underlying emotional responses which obviously add fuel to Neptune's escapist tendencies.

The positive pole of Neptune is that of the Higher Venus, the messenger of divine and compassionate love. To learn to forgive those who appear to do us wrong, and to rise above desire—whatever that desire is—is the message that needs to be recognized here. As Alice Bailey wrote, "Love is fallen and blinded when desire is rampant; desire vanishes when love triumphs."[3] Neptune can exemplify escapist tendencies, and it is for this reason alone that we need to look at—and begin to recognize—love in its purest form. It is very hard for us to comprehend this, for we are brought up to think in other ways and to believe that desire *is* love; this is obviously something we must understand better. If we can only realize that it is when we are unhappy, or not at ease in some area, that we desire— not when we truly love.

Neptune-Venus aspects will certainly cause us to fall in love with love at times, and to project onto the other person, people, or situation a perfected image. When the truth is finally seen, a lot of hurt feelings on both sides will naturally ensue. A relationship built on this type of illusion is seldom happy or long-lasting after the initial Neptunian romanticism has worn off. If this kind of union is to survive, *love* must be more fully understood on other levels. These aspects cause a search for a *pure love*, but this cannot exist just within a physical concept, because it is purely a realization of the Soul.

---

[3] Alice Bailey, *Esoteric Astrology,* vol. 3, *Seven Rays* (New York: Lucis Publishing, 1965), p. 171.

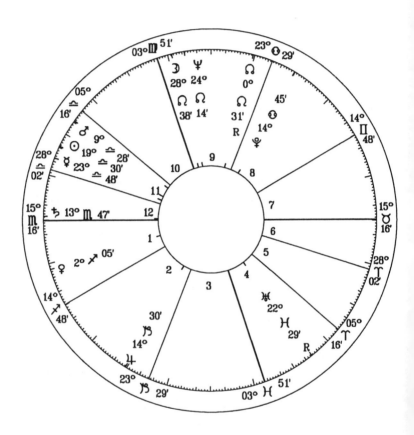

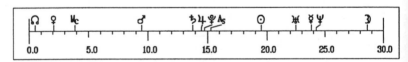

Chart 6. Margaret Thatcher's chart. October 13, 1925, 9:00 A.M. GMT. Grantham, England. Data from The Blackwell Data Collection, published by Astrolabe Placidus houses. Chart calculated by Astrolabe using Nova Printwheels.

If we look at the many combinations of love that Venus-Neptune aspects bring, we see they are drawing man and woman to a higher development of feelings, in some cases to a mystical understanding of love. In true mysticism, love and feelings are not sacrificed, but experienced at a more rarefied and higher level of awareness.

Venus-Neptune aspects may also bring in the platonic type of love relationship that requires no physical union, one that is bonded to a higher ideology. This can work if it fits happily into the real life of the two people, but if it is based completely on illusory factors it may not survive.

If we consider erotic love, and accept that a desire for sexual union is in natural connection with human biology and procreation, we find abstinence for the sake of religious or spiritual reasons can create its own negative whirlpool. The only real criterion within any marriage or close partnership is the need for a higher morality which recognizes a respect for all those connected within the relationship.

Love and sex within our materialistic society have almost become one, along with a lot of false concepts and glamor. Ideally they should exist together, but not in the way we are led to believe. The person who has given up false ideals and needs connected with love, and who is nearer to finding wholeness within himself or herself, is much more able to experience love than the unrealistic and undeveloped idealist.

Abraham Maslow[4] points out that "self actualizing people" can more easily take or leave an intimate sexual relationship than any other group, due to a wholeness within themselves, and that when they do enjoy sexual union it is with greater enjoyment than other such groups. This leads to an interesting point. It seems that everything we experience physically has a higher counterpart: to reach out to that, we must learn to love more—not desire, but love—no simple task. Love and the sexual act can become a supreme spiritual experience, but it must be from a wholeness within the personality and spirit rather than from any other factor.

*Being in love* can bring a lot of pain to some people, especially with the hard aspects between Venus and Neptune. They often pick seemingly unsuitable or unobtainable partners, and most of the time they are not satisfied even when they find someone willing to share their life with them.

---

[4] See Abraham Maslow, *Motivation and Personality* (New York: Harper & Row, 1970), p. 187.

So is it necessary to suffer through love? Most of us have no concept of what love is, and we equate it with the romanticism we have been brought up with. The ideal is often portrayed in literature, but we, with all our emotional hangups, cannot ever *love* in this *whole* way. This is why we feel so much pain and, because of our own emotional inadequacies, we long for wholeness through another person. *Being in love* can teach us how to grow, for through the pain it brings we may learn something of great value, but only if we will allow this learning to take place, as Kahlil Gibran writes:

> But if in your fear you would seek only love's peace and love's
>     pleasure,
> Then it is better for you that you cover your nakedness
>     and pass out of love's threshing floor,
> Into the seasonless world where you shall laugh,
>     but not all of your laughter,
> and weep, but not all of your tears.
> Love gives naught but itself and takes naught but from itself.
> Love possesses not nor would it be possessed;
> For love is sufficient unto love. [5]

This is what love gives us, naught but love! We suffer through the pain of our emotions when we want the other person to give us exactly what we need back—to feed our painful and often inadequate emotional natures. Love and affection can be understood much more when we can stand back from some of our own emotional pain.

Over the years I have met many patients suffering through love. Long after the other person has left, they remember them with longing and many times old relationships have stopped any real progress for future partnerships. It is possible, however, to work with this problem.

Neptune's exaltation is in Cancer, and Cancer is ruled by the Moon which governs our emotional nature; Neptune is also the esoteric ruler of Cancer, and I believe that, if the emotional nature is investigated, it can help enormously with hard Venus-Neptune aspects. If you read the chapter on Flower and Gem Remedies, (page 87) you will see they treat various problems, including deep, underlying emotional issues. By using them,

---

[5] Kahlil Gibran, "On Love," *The Prophet* (New York: Alfred A. Knopf, 1975), lines 34-43.

real insight into old emotional problems begins to develop, enabling the person involved to see any relationship issue more clearly and realistically. This is also of great help when seeing a counselor or therapist, as it gives much more ability to stand back and look at the feeling nature objectively. How the gem remedies work to help bring to the surface and transform our emotional deficiencies are discussed in chapter 11.

# 7

# SATURN, THE BASIS FOR UNDERSTANDING NEPTUNE

> [Neptune's] power for evil is great, and is due to its unreliable, unstable, changeful, undependable nature; lack of cautious self-control, and consequent liability to be led away by impulse, by love of sensation and emotion; its willingness to be dominated by a stronger mind; its unregulated sympathies; and its liability to undesirable forms of mediumship or psychism.
>
> —Alan Leo[1]

In astrology, the formless and insubstantial element of Neptune seems diametrically opposed to the concrete structure of Saturn. It seems that these planets must of necessity be a very uncomplimentary pair. Saturn is the god of time and of earthly existence, matter in its structural form, and yet within the planetary system Saturn stands between the personal planets and the transpersonal planets of which Neptune is one. Saturn can be used as a bridge, as it were, between the two groups—an overpass formed between Heaven and Earth.

Saturn is the basis for all spiritual development in the truest sense. Saturn is the god of karma—of limitations and necessary lessons. If these lessons are not fully understood and worked through thoroughly, pain ensues, and this pain and limiting influence is a fertile breeding ground for Neptune's escapist tendencies, which can manifest in many diverse and ambiguous ways. These include drug taking, alcohol abuse, religious delusions and low-grade spiritualism and psychism, mental and moral

---

[1] Alan Leo, *The Art of Synthesis* (Edinburgh: International Publishing Co., 1949), pp. 108, 109. This title has been reissued by Inner Traditions, Rochester, VT.

aberrations, chaotic reasoning, cunning, deceitfulness, fearful imaginings, false concepts and representation, and also the more negative martyr-like tendencies. These, of course, are Neptune's lower attributes, but they may sometimes occur even when Neptune is well aspected, especially when triggered off by transit.

Until Saturn's responsibility is comprehended as fully as possible and worked with on both an inner and outer level, Neptune will continue to weave deceptive fantasies, generating false and deluded needs and desires which will then continue to enslave the lower ego until the negative basis for them is unearthed. Neptune's more malefic attributes must not be side-stepped, but they cannot be recognized for what they are until the more structured message from Saturn's placement is recognized, for Neptune affects us on different levels, as Alan Leo explains.

> Acting on the physical plane and in the body of man, it produces all kinds of excitement for which there is little real cause, instability in the fortunes, a fickle celebrity, fame liable to reversal . . . .

> On the psychic or emotional plane of life, it affects the subject with extreme excitability and changefulness of emotion and desire. It leads to an undue enthusiasm that allows the feeling to get upper hand of the judgment . . . .

> On the mental plane, and when affecting the mental rulers, Neptune conduces to shallowness of character, simulation, conscious deception or aptness for all kinds of intrigues, and disposes to short sighted acts of misrepresentation. It tends to enslave the intellect with every new phase of opinion, and makes the mind fickle, deceptive, disposed to imitation, plagiarism and even forgery . . . .[2]

Neptune is fluid and reflective like water and will mirror the birth chart according to its make-up and character. In the chart of one individual the more negative characteristics of Neptune would manifest, while in the chart of a person with a more developed nature, even the difficult aspects would do less harm, although there may still be more negative sensitivity than usual.

---

[2] Alan Leo, *The Art of Synthesis*, pp. 109, 110.

Until our own limitations are acknowledged with responsibility, Neptune's universal and all-embracing love of god and human cannot exist. The reason for this is simple. If we feel limited and oppressed, the blame is usually put on something outside ourselves and, while this continues to happen, we show that we have not accepted our own limitations as a means for growth and learning. As this negative pattern generates an increasing need of separateness from others, so Neptune's energy is more likely to be used in some form of escapism, engendering false concepts and values, rather than in seeing and feeling oneself in harmony with all things.

It is possible for people to appear loving and kind—as the "flower power" people did, for example—when there is still much lower-mind delusion present and a great deal of negative impulse. So how do we learn to work with this god? Only through Saturn can the message be heard. Only through Saturn can the beautiful ideals of true compassion and understanding for our fellow human beings be realized, for many wrong paths may be trod in search of the Neptune ideal.

When the Neptunian dream only brings suffering—which it often does—the person involved may become very bitter, wondering why he or she seems so often thwarted by life, and why others always manage so easily to get what they want. This again is only lower mind delusion, and a false and negative image. Every time this happens we need to ask ourselves the question: WHY? And this question can only be answered by understanding the Saturn and Neptune placements in the natal chart. For until lower mind delusion is recognized for what it is, the veil of maya[3] will continue to wrap itself around our senses, and delude us into believing many unrealities, and this can include certain issues connected to spiritual or psychic development.

Until the personality has obtained some degree of balance, the development of any special spiritual or psychic ability should not be attempted. In Eastern philosophy it is recognized that we must first find ourselves before we can lose ourself. This means that the base and core of the individual's personality must indeed be very solid before he or she can immerse in any type of cosmic state. The potential danger was recognized in the East and the aspirant was usually guided by a spiritual teacher. Now in our modern age that teacher can be within ourselves—but only if we truly recognize Saturn's message.

---

[3] Alan Leo says *maya* is illusion, the cosmic power which renders phenomenal existence possible. See *The Art of Synthesis*, p. 269.

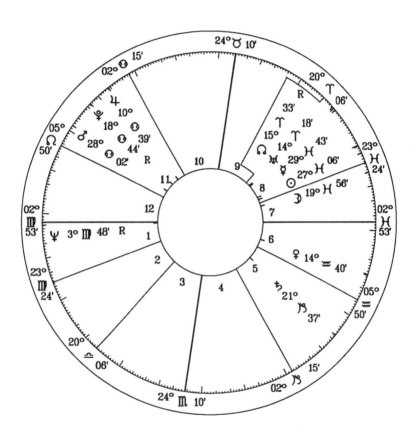

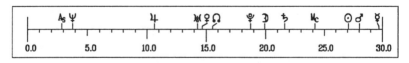

*Chart 7. Robert's chart. Birth data from family has been withheld for confidentiality. Placidus houses. Chart calculated by Astrolabe using* Nova Printwheels.

There are many people with extremely sensitive charts, and they need to express this sensitivity in a positive way rather than suffer from its negative connotations. The meditation with Saturn (on page 71), is designed to help with any problem, including those connected to Neptune.

Chart 7 shows Neptune in the 1st house conjunct the Ascendant, and there are six planets in water signs. Robert,[4] a successful artist, and until his first illness a professional man, has suffered a negative and sometimes incapacitating disturbance from psychic sources in the past, almost as though his abundant creativity could not be contained within a normal life style. He had worked extensively with Saturn over a period of a few months—which brought a great deal more stability and firmness to his nature. He is very idealistic, keen to work on his relationship problems and anxious to be free of the negative psychic influences which have caused so many problems in the past.

On his journey to Saturn he takes the gift of a plaster figure representing his egoistic illusory self. This is an act which represents his desire to give up his false sense of being and doing. He also asks the following questions.

1) How can I give up my false and illusory self and learn to live from the Heart?

2) Please explain why I spend so much time chasing pointless things that have no value?

3) How can I take a hundred percent responsibility for my life?

4) I want to ask about psychism—and what should my attitude be toward it?

## THE MEDITATION

I reach the temple and look through a grill on the door to see the gatekeeper—he reminds me of myself. He is dressed in a white caftan and turban.

---

[4] See also Neptune—Case Histories, p. 77, and *The Saturn/Pluto Phenomenon*, pp. 55, 154.

Inside the temple it is dark, there is a groaning murmur as if they are saying prayers. The area immediately inside the door which is right at the back of the temple is packed. People stand shoulder to shoulder, eyes closed, their faces raised to heaven.

I look about and notice I am very relaxed—a new experience—I have confidence in this place. There are several people here that I know. I feel rather concerned over this; I must ask Saturn about this.

I move through the crowd and notice a large balcony hangs overhead, making this place dark—but it gets lighter as I walk toward Saturn, although he is still a long way off. He really does seem a long way away. I walk over the black and white tiled floor with black open squares on white. I walk on, then up three steps until I stand before him.

"I am happy and pleased to be here," I say in greeting.

If we were standing he would be about ten feet tall; for some reason his almost human size fills me with pleasure and hope. He radiates health and magnetic energy, he is very relaxed and friendly, he smiles.

He has luxuriant straight hair gathered behind beneath a crown—like Alfred's—the crown is simple and lead-colored. He wears a tunic—pale gray with a purple key pattern at the hem, sleeve, and neck. Bare legs and Roman sandals.

I give him my gift—the plaster figure of myself. He looks at it without judgment, in mock admiration and affection, and asks, "What are we to do with it?"

"Smash it," I say.

"Very well," replies Saturn, forming his right hand into a fist and bringing it down heavily, powdering the figure to dust.

I feel pain and regret that it must go; but go it must.

"Very well," says Saturn, "out of the dust shall we form a true Self." He forms the dust into a cup—a grail cup—and lifts it lovingly, placing it within my heart.

"Now the question you wish to ask me?" says Saturn.

"I think you may have already answered it Saturn!" I say this before I ask, and then add, "I am so cut off from feeling, and unable to know how to feel. I

THE URANUS-NEPTUNE INFLUENCE / 57

understand something of life. I understand my desire to be responsible—
but I see this as avoiding feelings, fearing they will be too strong. How do
I learn to live from the heart and Love?"

SATURN: Well, know that your desire will be answered.
Love is all our concern.
And that love of the Self—the Christ love—is for all.
Never look back. Never look back.
Go forward, think more from the heart, not the head.
But be not too hard on your head—it has brought you here.
Welcome feelings long since buried;
let them live, let them go,
to be replaced by more real, heartfelt being.
Change comes in strange ways, unexpected, unexplained.
Be a child again; start where you left off.
Life is before you full of hope and trust.

I ask him why I spend so much time doing pointless things that really have
no value.

SATURN: The trap is in the desire to do.
To get out of the trap requires courage and conviction.
The one you have, the other grows.
Persevere, go on letting it grow.
Activity will flow.
Erase "doing" from your thoughts,
work at it, do not give up.
It will come and the nightmare will be over.
One thing, do not look back.

QUESTION: I wish to take a hundred percent responsibility for my life—
to heal the truth—and I need guidance on how to do this?

SATURN: Karmically you are taking full responsibility for your life, the
sooner you realize this the better, and the sooner the healing. It is about discrimination. How do you know? Trust your Self.[5] Straight is the gate, and
narrow the path. Always follow your conscience. Sincerity leads us to the

---

[5] The higher part of the Higher Mind.

Truth. Be alone, that alone you may Be. In that Being is the key to all. It is simple. From your Being love all. In the loving of all is the healing of the earth—and all time.

QUESTION: What should my attitude be towards psychism?

SATURN: Good, you are not so afraid.
Your alarm I understand—
you are not without help and protection.
Come more often with these problems.
You will be confronted with this until you resolve it.
But you can always say No! at any moment.
There's all the time you need.
Go carefully—observe; note; question;
think; sense—and ask.
Everything has its place—
find that place and keep it there.
Be not afraid; all is well.

I ask about an explanation of "psychism" given to me by a spiritualist medium.

SATURN: It may be right—but what of it?
Trust yourself.
Go nowhere you do not feel happy
and confident to go—within or without.

I become Saturn. I feel his strength and absolute authority. His energy compacted. I see Robert as a child. My heart and concern are full of love and protection for this little soul. I feel irritation and exasperation for those fears unwilling to come forward. But also I feel a certain indifference to them. Let them stay—what matters it? In the fullness of time all will come. I feel that I am here to work to serve the great plan which is in my possession. This I share with others, to whom I give my instinctive love and support.

I feel for the child which is Robert and make a present of armor that he may be protected, and angels that will accompany him. I give him the gift of a little figure—it is a black knight. I feel relieved as I experience Saturn's energy. I become myself again and feel full of energy and hope. I see a lot of energy around him. I say goodbye.

The gatekeeper is the same—and lovingly concerned for me.

So Robert continues to work to bring the fullness of his abundant creative powers into positive manifestation, to be used as intended in love and strength through his own unique purpose on earth. He learns to unfold naturally, learning there is autumn, as well as other different seasons, and within life all are equally important.

# 8

# THE NEPTUNE
# EXERCISE AND MEDITATION

By clearly imagining a possibility, we automatically bring it closer to actualisation. Therefore, we can intentionally use images to aid our purpose in coming into full, embodied existence. And we can do so by thinking of the next appropriate step in our personal evolution.

—Piero Ferrucci[1]

Neptune's position on the chart will indicate an area of experience that is often unfocused, evasive, and vague. As will be seen by the case histories in chapter 10, Neptune's hidden message may be realized through allowing impressions to evolve through our feelings, our senses, and our intuition. It is important when doing the meditation, to follow the instructions given, and thus to use the meditation in the way intended, for as Neptune is involved it is very easy to be led astray.

Always work first to understand, integrate, and develop strengths from Saturn and the Saturn Meditation before attempting to work with Neptune. If you do have any difficulty with the Neptune Meditation, take these difficulties back again to Saturn and request help to work through the problems.

When working with the Neptune Meditation, you begin to realize that not all of your ideals may be realized at the present time. For instance you may find that some of your lesser ideals are sacrificed to a greater ideal, or, sometimes the opposite may be true. Occasionally you may find that one ideal will work against the realization of another, and it will be for you to choose which ideal is most important to you at this time.

---

[1] Piero Ferrucci, *What We May Be* (Wellingborough, England: Turnstone Press, 1982), p. 166.

*Please also note the following when using Part 2 of the Neptune Meditation:*

• Certain elements that you experience during the Neptune Meditation will change periodically due to transits or progressions, although the main theme will usually stay the same.

• If you start to see clear images in the underwater scene that take your attention away from the meditation, or you start to work with a Neptunian figure, as you would with the Saturn Meditation, then you are not in the Neptunian space intended.

• The aim of the meditation is to allow images from the unconscious to flow within the mirrors—the mirrors themselves will contain the message—and other experiences, seen outside of the mirrors, must be recognized as just Neptunian digression.

Part 1 is an exercise to bring into conscious awareness spiritual and idealistic parts of the nature, so that they may be recognized, accepted, and integrated into daily life. Part 2 involves inner work in the form of a meditation. Look at the following exercise—Part 1—The Ideal, and write it down in a wide awake state. By recognizing our ideals and wishes, we can more objectively identify with these, hitherto rather vague, parts of our personality.

## PART 1: THE IDEAL

1) Now imagine an Ideal—the most perfect life you can visualize. Everything you want is here. The only work here is that which gives you pleasure and happiness.

2) Imagine your own house; is it the one you have now, or different? If so, how different—and how is it more perfect?

3) Who would your partner be? Is it the partner you have now, or someone you know, or an imaginary figure? Or would you choose to be alone?

4) Imagine visiting an ideal friend, or friends—you may know them or not. Notice how they live, their life-style, how they use their time. Note

their sensitivity to beauty. Talk with them, see what is their way of thinking. Look at their home, the things they love surrounding them.

5) Imagine how you would be in this world. What gifts, attributes, or qualities would you like to see in yourself? Think of yourself in the most perfect way you can. What makes you happiest in this perfect world— and is it possible there is something you do not like?

Out of the above exercise, what is the most important Ideal you have? Make notes and be as explicit as possible.

NOTE: This exercise may be difficult, and it could take some time before it can be properly formalized and detailed. If possible, take some time to recognize your ideals fully before going on to the following Neptune Meditation.

## PART 2: THE NEPTUNE MEDITATION

Take your one most important Ideal from Part 1 and work with the following meditation.

To do the meditation sit or lie down in a comfortable position. Relax yourself thoroughly from the top of your head to the tips of your toes. It is a good idea to put the following meditation on a cassette tape.[2]

Imagine a beach, anywhere in the world.
A beautiful beach with miles and miles of soft white sand.
A blue sky above you, and the Sun shining immediately overhead,
    not hot, or burning, but comfortably warm.
The sea is a lovely turquoise, reflecting the Sun's rays.
So clear and clean you can see right down into it.
Imagine standing on the edge of the sea shore,
    then walk into the clear warm waters,
and dive down under the water into the crystal clear ocean.

---

[2] Or see Resources in the Appendix.

You dive down into the fathomless depths.
The water is clear.
Everywhere there is a shimmering luminosity,
A faint turquoise haze drifts in and out of the underwater view.
You may see coral, ocean plants and ferns.
Be aware of the many images that make up this underwater scene.
You dive still further into the underwater depths.
Eventually your feet come to rest on the ocean bottom.

You see fishes swimming by.
You look around you.
You are standing in an underwater city.
There are many streets and houses, an inn and market.
A church beckons its would-be brethren.
Fishes swim in and out of the windows and doorways
      of both hovel and mansion.

In the distance you see a shimmering, translucent castle.
Its structure is made up entirely of thought forms.
Its walls misty and hazy.
The doors are the same, and waver in the hazy green light.
Enter into the castle.
You find yourself in some sort of great hall.
Inside everything is slightly unclear.
You think there may be people there, but they are indistinct.
You may imagine you see a figure there,
      sitting on a shell-like throne.
The images change and waver in this unreal realm.
How do you feel as you experience this?

On one wall of the great hall there are three great mirrors.

Take your most important Ideal and see an image
      of this appear in the first mirror.
Try to see it as clearly as possible.
What is it that you see?
What do you feel?
Does the image change as you view it? If so, how?

Look closer to see what happens as you view your Ideal.
Is this Ideal what you really would like?

*Imagine standing on the edge of the sea shore, then walking into the clear warm waters, and diving under the water into the crystal clear ocean.*

Move on to the second mirror.
In this mirror, see your material world,
the world you live in now on earth.
What element in the material world
	stands between you and your Ideal?
See the material aspect of your life clearly.
What exactly do you see?
Does the image change at all as you look at it?
What are your feelings as you look at the image in the mirror?

Move to the third mirror.

See in this mirror an image which shows compromise
	or balance between the Ideal and reality.
What do you see?
How are you feeling?

Try and see the balance clearly.
How do you feel as you view your compromise—
	are you content with the result?
If not content, why?

Look around you in this ethereal, watery palace.
What do you see?
How do you feel?

Go back outside onto the ocean bed.

On the ocean floor you will see a treasure chest.
Inside this chest is something of great value to you.
Lift the lid and find your gift.
What is it? It may be symbolic.
What does it mean to you?
What do you feel as you look at it?
Bring this gift back with you into the material world.

Then, in your own time, let your consciousness drift back into your own
room, and open your eyes.

Write down your experiences, as the details may quickly be forgotten.

*You dive still further into the underwater depths. Eventually your feet come to rest on the ocean bottom.*

*You may imagine a figure there, sitting on a shell-like throne. The images change and waver in this unreal realm. How do you feel as you experience this?*

Make notes on the meditation experience. Does it seem you are overly idealistic in some area, or are your ideals balanced within your life's structure? If you experience difficulty between the ideal and the reality of your life's situation, take the resulting problem to Saturn. Work with Saturn to understand the best way to balance your areas of frustration and difficulty.

# 9

# THE SATURN MEDITATION

Saturn is the great sifter in human evolution. Metaphorically speaking, none may pass the influence of this planet who have not paid the debts of fate, or Karma, to the uttermost farthing. In every crisis, and in all critical stages of man's evolution, the influence of Saturn decides the issue. Saturn is, therefore, the planet of pure Justice, holding the scales of Libra, the perfect balance. This planet is Judge and Law-giver and represents the Justice of God.

—Alan Leo[1]

The frustrating experiences which are connected with Saturn are obviously necessary as they are educational in a practical as well as a psychological sense. Whether we use psychological or esoteric terminology, the basic fact remains the same: human beings do not earn free will except through self-discovery, and they do not attempt self-discovery until things become so painful that they have no other choice.

—Liz Greene[2]

To do the following meditation, sit or lie down comfortably and relax as deeply as possible. You can make note at different points throughout the meditation or wait until you have finished. When doing the meditation, I use a cassette tape and pause it at different points of interchange to make

---

[1] Alan Leo, *Esoteric Astrology* (London: N. Fowler & Co., 1925), p. 26.
[2] Liz Greene, *Saturn: A New Look at an Old Devil* (York Beach, ME: Samuel Weiser, 1976), p. 11.

notes, but everyone should find the way that is easiest and the most con-
venient for them.

Further details in regard to Saturn's influence on the human condition, including Saturn by sign and house, working with the Saturn meditation, case studies and questions and answers, are contained in *The
Saturn/Pluto Phenomenon*.[3]


## THE MEDITATION

Imagine a very cold country.
The landscape is bleak-barren.
The sky is gray—there's a cold icy mist.
And there are dark forbidding mountains in the distance.

You feel cold and shivery.
Heavy and tired.
There's no one there—it's lonely and cold.

An icy wind whips around you.
Your body aches—you feel tired and weary
But you walk onward toward the mountains.

As you get nearer to the mountains
You see snow in patches on them
And mist around their craggy peaks.

You walk on for some time
And eventually reach the lower slopes of the mountains.
Now there are boulders on the path—the way is difficult
But you persevere.
You feel so cold and lonely
You press on.

You climb over stones
And edge your way around boulders.
Now you see a path that leads up

---

[3] *The Saturn/Pluto Phenomenon* (York Beach, ME: Samuel Weiser, 1993).

To the huge gray cold mountain.
You start to climb,
Your legs ache—and the air is getting colder.

Stop and look below—notice how high you have climbed.
Continue, even though you are weary.

Now you walk into a thick cold mist—you cannot see.
Just edge forward inch by inch.
You may trip and fall—feel your way with your hands.
You struggle through the mist—not knowing where you are
Or where you are going.
You continue feeling lonely and lost.
The mist thins.
You see a huge plateau.
There is still a lot of mist.

Rising from the mist is a huge black stone temple.
This is the place you wanted to find.

You walk to the door—the sky seems darker.
Knock on the door—which is opened by the gatekeeper.
What does he look like?—What is he wearing?
How do you feel about him?

He will ask you what you want.
Tell him why you are there—why you want to see Saturn.
He may answer—or he may just let you in.

When inside, you are shown into a huge hall—
there are people there.
The ceilings are high—the hall long.
Look at the people—what they wear—how they are behaving.
How do you feel about them?

At the other end of the hall you see a huge stone throne.
There is a large figure on the throne.
It is Saturn—the God Kronus.
Walk up to him.
Look up at him—notice how he sits—
how he holds his arms and hands.

Can you see what he wears?
Can you see his face?
Does he have anything on his head—
What is his hair like?
How does he make you feel?

Ask him if he will work with you and be your friend.
Tell him why you're there—what you want.
How you want him to help you.
Give him the gift you have brought for him.
It may be anything—it may be symbolic.
Does he accept it?

Ask him anything else you may wish to—
and listen to his reply

Notice how you feel.

Now imagine walking out of your own body—
And walking into the body of Saturn.
You become the God sitting on his throne.
You take on his shape and form.
Feel yourself in his body—looking out of his eyes at you.

How do you see yourself—do you like what you see?
How do you see the others in the hall?—
some you may know.

Give a gift to the person in front of you
Who has come to ask for your help.
How can you help this person on their journey?

As you sit on the throne feel your strength—
Your responsibility.
Feel your power and ability to help the person in front of you—
And the others in the hall.
Realize what you are feeling is your own energy—
your own strength.
And anytime you choose you can experience this feeling.
For a moment or two, experience taking on your full power—
Using your full positive Saturn energy.

Note how you feel.

After experiencing this energy,
Step back out of the God
And back into your own body—
Become you again.
When this is done turn and look at Saturn.
Is he different?—Do you feel any different?

Thank him for seeing you.
Ask if you may come back to see him
and speak to him again.
If you wish to say any final words to him do so—
And listen to his reply.

When you have finished say Good-bye.

Walk down the hall to the door.
Is the gatekeeper the same—or has he changed?
How do you feel about him?

Walk outside.
Perhaps the Sun is starting to shine.
And the clouds are moving away.

Walk across the plateau
And take the path down the mountain.
The mist is almost gone.
As you walk down you may see tiny flowers
Starting to blossom in the rock's crevices.

Perhaps the long long winter is nearly over.

Walk down the mountain.
As you walk down
Let your consciousness come back into your own room.
And open your eyes.

# 10

# NEPTUNE—
# CASE HISTORIES

> We should find perfect existence through imperfect existence.
>
> —Shunru Suzuki[1]

The following case histories show how, by working with the Neptune Meditation, unresolved problem areas and conflicts can develop more clarity and understanding. The Neptune Meditation may be used on anybody who has worked with the Saturn Meditation, including children. It is particularly useful for focusing blind spots within the personality, whether we use the Meditation on ourselves—or as in the case of counselors—on our clients.

The meditation may evolve in a very simple way, especially when working with children, as shown in the following case history of Simon, or, as in the case of Robert, it may be revealingly complex. But, however it presents itself, it will throw greater light and clarity on our ideals, as well as how Neptune influences us on many hidden and diverse levels.

Simon was a very grown up 12-year-old, whose mother brought him for therapy because of depression that made him very tearful and generated certain suicidal feelings and thoughts. He explained his feelings of depression as a heavy blanket weighing him down. He was a sensitive and friendly boy, from a home that was caring, supportive, and very academic. Due to the depression, several months of schooling had been lost.

Simon's birth time was exact, his Sun was conjunct Pluto in Libra but unaspected by other planets, Venus was conjunct his Virgo Ascendant.

---

[1] Shunru Suzuki, *Zen Mind, Beginner's Mind* (New York: Weatherhill, 1985), p. 102.

Saturn was also in Libra in the 2nd house, conjunct Jupiter in Virgo; Saturn sextiled Mars, and Jupiter was conjunct the Moon. Neptune, however, in the 4th house, was square both Moon and Jupiter, and sextiled Pluto. The 4th house also contained a Mars-Uranus conjunction. Harmony was obviously very important to Simon, but he had both Saturn and Pluto in Libra to contend with. Neptune in difficult aspect to his Moon-Jupiter conjunction could make him very idealistic with regard to his home life, and to the possibility of his being over kind and generous to others. See Chart 8 on page 80.

Simon took to therapy well, and was both responsive and imaginative; his mother sat in on all of his sessions. His mother said she thought the depression had developed because his best friend at school (it was the school's policy that everyone had to have a best friend) was very vindictive and spiteful toward him. However, he had several other good friends at school whom he got on well with and who shared his love of animals; and he belonged to several wildlife protection societies. A first visit was made to Saturn.

## FIRST VISIT TO SATURN

A knight in armor opened the door of Saturn's Temple and showed Simon into a long, cold room with paintings on the wall. The people in the hall were like ghosts in old fashioned clothes. He felt out of place and did not like the people there.

I asked him what the people were doing; he said some were thinking, and some were dancing, and there were some children standing by a fire. As he looked at the hall it became warmer and more pleasant.

Saturn was sitting on a throne at the top of some steps, a red carpet led to the throne. He was short, fat and had lots of rings, and was about 50 years old. He had brown hair and a beard, and wore a crown. He seemed friendly, and held a golden stick.

I asked Simon how he felt; he said, "I feel small as if I'm not wanted there, and I feel as though he cannot see me."

But as he stood looking up at Saturn, he said he began to feel an excitement inside, almost a happy feeling was developing. Simon's gift to Saturn is a stone; Saturn thanks him; he puts it on a string around his neck. Saturn tells him he can stay there forever. Simon said he feels very wanted.

He then becomes Saturn, wanting to help Simon, and feeling sorry for him. He says Simon is not like the others in the hall, he needs more help, adding that the others have already had help.

Becoming Simon again, he said it was good to know what it felt like to be the god. Simon also recognized, on leaving the hall, that the others accepted him, and that he felt a lot more comfortable.

## SECOND VISIT TO SATURN

The gatekeeper is different, he is young and in modern dress, black hair drawn back in a pony tail. Simon remarks that it is strange finding him here. He tells the gatekeeper that he has come back to see Saturn, and the gatekeeper tells him to go in.

The people in the hall are wearing old-fashioned clothes; Simon feels happy and accepted, as if he has gained their friendship. Saturn is the same. He is happy; tells Simon that he is like him; Simon feels excited.

Simon has brought flowers from his world to the world of Saturn; they are red roses; Saturn takes them. Simon says he feels warm and cared for. Simon becomes the god, and says he is glad to help someone. Sees himself as a little older and dressed in winter clothes, he is happy and a little more confident.

As Saturn he says, "I do not really know Simon very well. I give him a ring for his memory so he will remember me." As Saturn he also says it is sometimes difficult to be in charge.

Over the next few weeks Simon's confidence visibly grew, he slept better and only experienced one or two brief periods of depression, which quickly passed. He returned to school, and school life quickly improved, he

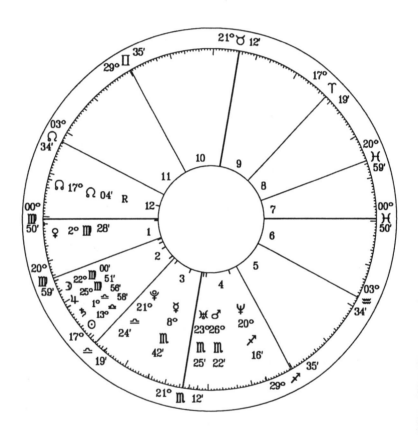

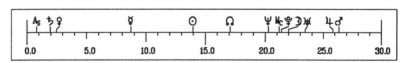

Chart 8. Simon's chart. Birth data from family has been withheld for confidentiality. Placidus houses. Chart calculated by Astrolabe using Nova Printwheels.

worried much less about his difficult friend. He did, however, admit to not being completely happy about having to go to school (natal Pluto in the 3rd house, indicating school before high school) and far preferred to be at home. Simon's chart showed Neptune in the 4th house, and so it was decided to do the Neptune Meditation to help clarify present conditions and feelings.

## NEPTUNE MEDITATION—THE IDEAL

1) The Ideal life Simon would like to live was on a big fertile desert island with lots of horses and different animals.

2) Simon's ideal home was a big old house with lots of rooms. In the house would be dogs cats and big aquariums. Also family, friends, or anyone else who didn't have a home.

3) The Ideal partner we did not investigate.

4) His friends would be all the friends he has now, as well as new ones he has not yet met.

5) Simon imagined how he would like to be himself. He wanted to be helpful to others, but strong.

Everyone getting on together makes him the happiest. His most important Ideal was to be strong, confident and helpful to others.

## THE NEPTUNE MEDITATION

Simon experienced the underwater scene like a dream world, very pretty. Someone rather vague was on a throne in the hall.

1) *The 1st Mirror*
(The most important Ideal)

The ideal that Simon saw in the first mirror was people laughing, singing, and talking; he was with these people feeling happy, strong, and confident. As he looked the image stayed the same.

2) *The 2nd Mirror*
(The Material World)

Simon said, "The material world I know is still here. I see my home, my home is happy and good, the only time I ever worry is if anyone is ill. My animals and my friends fit my ideal as well. But school does not fit in my world, without school life would be perfect."

Simon then looks at the image of school to see why he doesn't like it. He saw that at school he enjoyed most of the work, he got on well and liked the teachers, there was no real problem with his difficult friend now. He added that although there were no real problems, school life may be connected to a feeling that in school there was a lack of love and safety.

3) *The 3rd Mirror*
(Compromise and Balance between the Ideal and the Material)

Simon said the compromise seemed to be learning from home with a private tutor (the family were in a position to have a private tutor, and in fact this had been discussed by them). However, it was decided, when seen in clearer perspective by Simon, that, although he would feel safer and more loved at home, there were too many nice things at school to be missed, particularly his friends. He realized he couldn't have everything exactly as he wanted it, but now had more confidence in himself and decided to settle for things as they were (natal Neptune sextile Pluto).

Simon's mother brings him for a therapy session when Simon feels the need. He continues to grow in strength and confidence.

The next example of working with the Neptune Meditation is Robert's work. See Chart 7 page 54, and pages 55–59 and 154–159 of *The Saturn / Pluto Phenomenon*. Robert has Neptune conjunct the Ascendant in Virgo in the 1st house, and semi-square Pluto in Cancer in the 11th. He has Sun, Moon and Mercury in Pisces and altogether six planets in water signs. The following example of working with the Neptune Meditation is in Robert's own words.

# NEPTUNE PART 1: THE IDEAL

1) (The most perfect life you can visualize, with work that gives pleasure and happiness):

An ideal life would be a perfect life. My first response is that I can't visualize it. Why? Because—it is beyond me. I'm not good enough, able enough, to know . . .

In my work I would be creative with ease; inspired, unhesitating, brilliant and original. An unending flow of work; satisfying and reassuring; my work recognized. A high level of skill and sensibility, with an excellent color sense.

In an ideal life I would be perfectly balanced, completely in touch with mind, feelings, body and the unconscious. My grasp on "true " reality would be firm and sure—I would be in "no doubt." My relationships with people would be easy and sure, satisfying and deeply fulfilling, but without dependency. Trusting but clear sighted.

I realize I'm describing my present life perfected—not a different one, but more—much more of the same . . . Suppose I try and visualize something quite different, great power and wealth for example, with a charismatic presence to influence people? That's intoxicating but not ideal. Perfect perhaps, but only momentarily. Whereas I can imagine my life "perfectly perfect" without all of these things to get in the way. Maybe perfection is about perfectibility, making more perfect.

2) Visualize the perfect house I find much easier. It would be a nice house in the countryside, old, with old-fashioned furniture and an old established garden. Attached to the house is a large studio, light and airy.

3) Visualizing the ideal partner I find more difficult, there is a certain resistance within me. A woman, intelligent, sensitive, aware, devoted to me. Tolerant of myself. An imaginary figure.

4) My ideal friend would be liberal, agreeable. Female, although sex is clearly not important. Intellectually stimulating, emotionally sympathetic.

Aware, with a spiritual dimension to things. There may be two friends, their conversation compassionate, deep, warm, intelligent, brief and to the point, humorous. Their thinking informed, logical, open-minded, showing understanding.

5) How would I be in this ideal world? I try to think of myself as I, ideally, would like to be. I would be confident and strong, understanding this world and my place in it. Successful, respected, authoritative, warm, humorous and compassionate. At ease with others, enjoying their company, feeling very much at one with life. Intensely involved with life, and without doubt. My life would be rich, full, meaningful and positive. I would be without want or limitation, able to travel and experience all of life's richness and meaning. At ease with all and interested by everything. What makes me happiest is being part of life and experiencing life. I think my ideal is really just more perfection in my work and present life.

## PART 2: THE NEPTUNE MEDITATION

I find I am swimming; it is cool and restful. I come to stand unsteadily on the ocean's bed. I notice gentle but strong currents. I walk slowly on through this strange atmosphere, witnessing it rather like a dream. Occasionally a silent form moves gently across my path and into my largely unfocused vision.

I see the underwater city, nothing is clear or sharp. I walk through the streets which feel wide but seem narrow. I move toward the castle, which I cannot see clearly—it is there and it is not. Now I mount three steps to the door, which I am aware of but do not see. It is slightly darker inside, but with iridescent areas of localized light which are moving.

I am now in a large area—it is like an enormous gothic cathedral, with aisles and fluted columns which rise up and then disappear. Everything is seen through a mist, nothing is definite to the eye, or to the touch. It is like looking at a reflection in water. It is even more dreamlike than a dream. Powerful, magnetic, palpable, but without substance.

It is slightly unnerving at first, I feel uneasy in this state of flux. I begin to accept it on its terms. I begin to move and glide through this place, even beginning to feel at home. The feeling now is not heavy, quite light in fact.

There is a presence at the other end of the hall. The image is there and not there. The substance I see is the thought. The more I allow the thought to be, the firmer the image becomes in it's own absence (for it was never there). The state of "hide and seek," which would normally unnerve me, is acceptable and causes no anxiety—I feel I can handle it.

*The 1st Mirror*
(The most important Ideal)

In the first mirror I see darkness, then a hand outstretched toward me, revealing in its palm a black cube. This comes into close-up. The cube opens, its inner surface is white. It lies flat, where it was is now space. Then a voice comes from the image. It says something to me about Saturn and the condition of time in realizing ideas.

"Go on," it says.

The hand changes position holding the now closed cube between index finger and thumb, "showing" me the cube clearly. The hand speaks of receiving images and ideas and making them manifest.

"This is your work," something says.

The image fades.

This feels reasonable, true. This Ideal seems to be the most important.

*The 2nd Mirror*
(The Material world)

I have difficulty "finding" an image. I then see an image of myself, I hear the image saying, "The material world is never good enough. The game is up, I know it is."

As I look at this image, I realize my own attitudes are the problem. I have to let certain attitudes go. In many ways my life is ideal. I know I need to be more confident, less afraid: to trust present conditions, working with them to transcend them, this is the only way.

I experience a feeling of irritation that it has taken me so long to realize such a simple thing; but I also experience relief—great relief as if a burden has been lifted.

*The 3rd Mirror*
(Compromise between the Ideal and the Material)

In the third mirror I see a reflection of the first image. I'm feeling calm and relieved. The Balance is clear. The only discontent is lack of money. Looking about it seems lighter—less dense, more clear—more acceptable as it is. More real in its own terms.


*The Chest*

The gift in the chest is a drawing block and white paper. To me it means I am in the right place, working, with the right materials. I feel reassured, relieved, thankful, strengthened by this confirmation.

# 11

# THE FLOWER
# AND GEM REMEDIES

> Let not the simplicity of this method deter you from its use, for you
> will find the further your researches advance, the greater you will
> realize the simplicity of all creation.
>
> —Edward Bach[1]

Neptune's role in therapy can be very elusive until the right way is found
to evaluate its unclear properties. Those with difficult aspects from Neptune
to personal planets—particularly the Sun or Mercury—may find it difficult
to recognize or work with certain parts of their personality. Neptune is our
blind spot, so we must try to recognize and work with the unconscious
area. As well as understanding Neptune's position and aspects on the natal
chart and working with the suggested exercises in chapter 8, there are
other ways to use the Neptunian influence, in healing for example.

The use of the Flower and Gem Remedies are two similar such ways.
It has been noticed that even those with very difficult aspects to Neptune
can benefit enormously from these remedies, as their very sensitivity causes
them to tune into this unique form of vibrational healing. These remedies
work through their ability to tune in to the subtle bodies of the intricate
human system. All the subtle bodies—or energy centers—send off a vibrational code; when this code is not functioning to its correct capacity for any
one of many diverse reasons, then a malfunction is felt which affects the bio-
molecular structure of the body and causes a dis-ease: this may manifest
itself in the mental, emotional or physical sphere. Each flower or gem

---

[1] Nora Weeks, *The Medical Discoveries of Edward Bach, Physician* (Saffron Walden, Essex,
England: C. W. Daniel, 1989), p.52.

essence has a particular resonance corresponding to specific parts of the body which resound at the same frequency, and they have been identified as causing positive psychological and physical changes to occur while that particular vibration is active. These remedies are a safe and sure way to assist humankind on its evolutionary path, a path which will never end while humans retain physical form, existing as it does through an endless spiral of life energy.

> The action of these remedies is to raise our vibrations and open up our channels for the reception of the Spiritual Self; to flood our natures with the particular virtue we need, and wash out from us the fault that is causing the harm. They are able, like beautiful music or any glorious uplifting thing which gives us inspiration, to raise our very natures, and bring us nearer to our souls and by that very act to bring us peace and relieve our sufferings. They cure, not by attacking the disease, but by flooding our bodies with the beautiful vibrations of our Higher nature, in the presence of which, disease melts away as snow in the sunshine.[2]

The flower remedies were introduced in this century by Dr. Edward Bach, a doctor of medicine who practiced for over twenty years in London as a bacteriologist and consultant. After he became interested in homoeopathy, he gave up his practice in 1930 to devote his time to researching the flower remedies, derived mostly from the flowers of wild plants, trees, and shrubs occurring naturally in the British Isles (olive is the exception).

He believed that a worry, fear, or other negative state of mind would deplete the body's energies, and thus the body would lose its natural resistance. He discovered flower remedies which cover 38 different negative states of mind, and these he clarified under seven headings: those for apprehension—for uncertainty and indecision—for lack of interest—for despondency and despair—for loneliness—for over-sensitivity—and for over-concern for the welfare of others. The remedies were safe and could be used by anyone with no harmful effects; they are now widely used and

---

[2] Edward Bach, *The Original Writings of Edward Bach* (Saffron Walden, Essex, England: C.W. Daniel, Ltd., 1990) p. 62.

available in most towns in the British Isles as well as being distributed throughout the world by the Bach Centre.

Similar flower essences are now available from the United States, but, other than having an inspirational link with Dr. Bach and his life's work, there is no other connection—the flower essences are unique. They are derived from a wide variety of plant species found in both North and Central America as well as other places throughout the world, and are used to treat a range of disorders. Examples include: *Bleeding Heart* for negative and possessive emotional attachments, allowing love to exist in freedom; *Buttercup* for appreciation of one's own self-worth; *Indian Paintbrush* for energy within creative expression: very useful for those doing creative work who seem to dry up; *Lotus* is a general spiritual remedy which uplifts and enhances meditation practices; *Mallow* is useful for over-coming insecurity in social conditions, and develops warmth within friend-ship. *Mountain Pride* gives strength in difficult situations, and allows active confrontation of evil or wrongdoing—spiritual warriorship; *Oregon Grape* helps cope with fear of emotional hostility from others; *Rabbitbrush* helps concentration on details, when your mind feels pulled in many directions at once; *Scotch Broom* shows obstacles as an opportunity for growth, and also helps where there is depression connected to the world situation; *Shooting Star* is for times when you feel not at home on earth, for soul alienation, brings a sense of belonging—good for astrologers; *Sunflower* is especially useful and can be used in combination with many other remedies; it bal-ances ego expression, and deals with problems caused by too little or too much self-esteem, bringing one nearer to the self; *Tansy* helps us to take decisive action to meet our goals; it also helps to develop will power.

The remedies work in a very safe and natural way, helping transform negative attitudes and emotions which impede positive development of the personality. They can also be particularly useful during difficult tran-sits and progressions, bringing more balance and perspective to the nature and personality.

It must be stressed here that for any of the remedies to work at their maximum potential, some responsibility upon the part of the recipient is required. For example, to take care of general health and diet—to devise some system for relaxation, however hectic the life-style—to try to set time apart for meditation or creative visualization—and, when necessary, to consult a qualified practitioner to assist with any problem area.

The following case history shows how it is possible to get maximum effects from the flower remedies. Jane was a young 11-year-old girl away at school; she strongly resented the fact she had to be away from home, particularly missing her mother and family pets. It was Jane's father who had insisted his daughter should have the best education he could afford, and his word seemed to be law. The situation at school was deteriorating rapidly, Jane was becoming argumentative, bad-tempered and very disruptive with both her fellow pupils and teachers.

After two therapy sessions with Jane and her mother, it seemed obvious some compromise needed to be reached. I asked Jane if she could have three wishes what they would be; and she replied she would like her mother to worry less, to be a day girl at school, and that her father would work less long and hard. It was decided by her family that if she co-operated and behaved at school during the week, she could come home every weekend—but only if her attitudes changed. Unfortunately her attitudes didn't change, she instigated more fights and arguments, both at school and home. Her father said if her behavior didn't change he would send her to another boarding school some two hundred and fifty miles away, and she would be very lucky to come home at half term, if then.

At the third session there seemed little time to work with the impending ultimatum, it was therefore agreed by Jane and her mother, who was very supportive, that a personal tape with suggestions that augmented both personal confidence and greater calmness should be made, and Jane would try and listen to this tape several times a week.

Just over a week later Jane's mother phoned to ask if I could do anything else to speed up the therapeutic process as the tape was not working rapidly enough. As Jane was away at school her mother had initially rejected the idea of the remedies. Now in desperation she contacted the school, and it was arranged that Jane should be allowed to take the medication four times a day while at school. The remedies were chosen mainly from a perusal of her natal chart. See Chart 9 on page 92. Jane took the following combination of remedies:

*Sunflower* to help with disturbances in her relationship with her father. Sunflower also helps balance the ego; it is good for the Sun in Leo or for those with Leo prominent (Sunflower is useful for many conditions, including difficult aspects to the Sun, or planets with difficult aspects in the fifth house.)

*Buttercup* to help Jane appreciate her self worth.

*Trumpet Vine* to help her articulate herself to others; it also helps protection of self in group or social situations, giving a healthy self assertion. (Mercury was in the 7th house square both Mars and Pluto in the 9th house and opposed the moon in the 1st. Mercury is also sextile Jupiter in the 8th and trine Uranus in the 10th).

*Vervain* for tension and being generally wound up.

*Chestnut Bud* for learning lessons from past mistakes.

*Mallow* for developing warmth in friendships, and for social insecurity.

*Oregon Grape* for fear of emotional hostility from others, also for incorrect perception of another's motives.

A dramatic improvement occurred within the first week of treatment, the teachers said Jane was like a different person, well-behaved, getting on much better with the other children. This improvement continued and grew. *Rabbitbrush* to help Jane's concentration at school was also added to the above remedies. Both home and family relationships improved, Jane joined the school's archery class, eventually becoming best within her group. In short all the negative reactions within Jane started to become much more positive, and instead of her behavior patterns having a negative connotation, on the contrary they became much more a positive strength. Jane took the remedies over several months. I only saw Jane on three occasions for therapy, her mother would phone for more remedies whenever her supply began to run out.

Ideally the remedies are used while therapy is in progress, but in any case where the patient is either uncooperative, or unable to attend regular therapy sessions—for whatever reason—the remedies can help bring in healing and a much greater sense of inner balance than was experienced before.

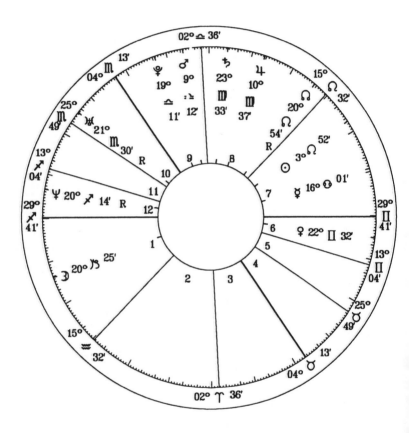

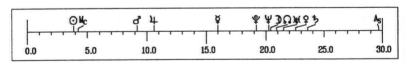

*Chart 9. Jane's chart. Birth data from family has been withheld for confidentiality. Placidus houses. Chart calculated by Astrolabe using Nova Printwheels.*

In addition to the Flower Remedies, there are the Gem Remedies. These fall somewhere in between the Flower Remedies, which work on the realms of the mind, and homeopathic preparations, which work closer to the physical body. The Gem Remedies can help deal with deep emotional problems as well as negative mental conditions; they can even help to alleviate physical pain or discomfort in some instances. For example, *Gold* and the flower remedy *Lotus* often ease pain in arthritic conditions. *Ruby* is very good for the eyes, particularly when used as an eye lotion. *Pearl* helps alleviate stomach conditions as well as bringing in more emotional stability.

Gemstones have been used in healing in a variety of different ways since time immemorial; these elixirs are certainly not new, but just a system of medicine which we, particularly in the West, have almost forgotten.

The gem remedy combinations listed below are particularly helpful with any Venus-Neptune aspects, including transits or progressions; they can also be helpful with hard progressed Moon aspects, particularly between the Moon and Pluto, and likewise transits between Pluto and/or the Moon and Venus. In fact they are helpful with any difficult aspect, transit, or progression involving the Moon and Venus. How the gem remedies work to help bring to the surface and transform our emotional deficiencies is discussed below.

The following gem remedy combinations are taken several times daily for four or five days. It should be noted that when very heavy transits or progressions are affecting the natal chart the contents of the emotions may also need the help of a therapist. In these cases it may appear that a healing crisis is occurring, but this is usually due to the hard aspects affecting the natal chart and can be a false interpretation of what is actually taking place.

The gem remedies are used in the following combinations. The first combination is *Malachite, Tiger's Eye* and *Dark Pearl*. This combination works on the deepest emotional levels. It will get to feelings unresolved since babyhood and early childhood. These are emotions that may be impossible to eradicate by orthodox therapy or counseling, and are connected to the two lowest chakras. As you take this remedy, buried feelings will rise to the surface to be faced. Tiger's Eye gives insight into these deep issues. Malachite eases nervous tensions and helps gastric problems. Dark Pearl restores peace where there is any deep emotional stress and anxiety. Take this remedy several times daily for four or five days.

The second combination is *Light Pearl*, *Tiger's Eye* and *Light Opal*, and works on the chakra connected to the solar plexus, opening up this level of the emotions. Light Pearl brings emotional issues nearer to the surface, where they can be faced with more confidence than ever before, due to the greater feeling of emotional wholeness beginning to pervade the personality. There can be much more clarity connected to the mother image and sometimes the family structure. Light Opal increases intuition and balances female qualities in both male and female. Take this remedy several times daily for four or five days following the first combination of remedies.

The third remedy is *Ruby* and *Turquoise* and brings in the ability to view past grievances and resentments within relationships. Sometimes these will rise as feelings of anger as old issues are faced, but they are then replaced by acceptance of the matter concerned and the ability to let go; feelings connected to the father and other figures of authority often come to the fore. Turquoise is known as a master-healer and brings peace of mind. Ruby is also a master-healer, particularly when connected to the father image, and balances the heart and heart chakra, bringing in the ability to change self-love into a more universal and all-embracing love. It gives stability and confidence as the heart opens and inner strength grows. Use this combination several times daily for four or five days following the second combination of remedies.

The fourth combination is *Lapis Lazuli*, *Malachite* and *Topaz*. Malachite continues to deal with any remaining emotional issues. Lapis Lazuli helps with any feelings of depression present and makes the mind clearer and so able to deal with any relevant issues. It stimulates the thyroid and helps ease tension and anxiety, it is connected to the throat chakra and so helps the person to communicate more openly, thus expressing true feelings. Topaz allows the person to work with the newly stabilized emotions, and Malachite makes sure all negative emotions have been eliminated. The Higher Self is activated. Take this combination several times daily for four or five days following the third combination.

The fifth combination of remedies consists of *Diamond*, *Clear Quartz* and *Rose Quartz*. Any remaining emotional negativity is released and deep insight into all emotional issues develops. There is enhanced receptivity to the higher vibrations of life, such as greater receptivity to beauty and the spiritual realms, as well as deeper clarity of thought as the Higher Self, which is our natural state, further awakens. Diamond will push any remaining negativity out into the subtle bodies. Rose quartz opens the heart and any false pride is negated, while personal creativity increases. Clear Quartz removes negative thought forms as well as elevating consciousness. Take this combination for four or five days following the fourth combination of remedies. The entire course may be repeated if it is felt necessary— each time you do this be aware of how you feel as you take the different combinations.

You can take the course several times if you feel the need: it can only enhance your life and relationships. Remember, visualization greatly helps the working of the remedies, as does adequate relaxation and rest, plus a good diet.

The use of the flower and gem remedies can help growth and awareness on all levels. Several references and the names and addresses of supplier are listed under Resources.

# 12

# URANUS IN MYTH, LEGEND, AND LITERATURE

> So father Ouranos put his children into the darkness of the Earth (material form) so that through Time (Saturn), they could learn to cope with increased voltages of truth. Thus they would not only remain alive but also be filled with added life. The Greek culture was a bit sanguine and so, naturally, are its metaphors. But we are the modern children of Ouranos and we are filled with the life-force of this deity which surges within us. We must, therefore, take care in our use of this power, for we are but evolutionary infants. We must make sure that we are well grounded by the lightning rod of Ouranos. Saturn, however, remains the symbol of the realization of our limitations and the teacher of the balanced understanding of material values.
>
> —Alan Oken[1]

Uranus—or Ouranus—was known to the ancients as the god of the sky or heaven. He coupled with his wife and mother, Gaia, who was the earth, and gave birth to the Titans of the Third race[2] who were personified by Saturn/Cronus. Within myth this signified the time when the Titans—who were created by the Will of God—were superseded by physical procreation. Gaia was angry with her husband, Uranus, because he kept his offspring locked in the dark of the earth and would not give them light—

[1] Alan Oken, *As Above, So Below Alan Oken's Complete Astrology* (New York: Bantam, 1980), pp. 217, 218.
[2] Madame Blavatsky *The Secret Doctrine*, vol. 2 (London: Theosophical Publishing House, 1928), p. 809.

*Saturn/Cronus, the god of time and structure born of the union between Uranus and Gaia, took rule over the earth (primal matter), which Uranus as the Creative Will had shaped into form and existence.*

this, it is said, was because he did not like what he had created—so she asked Cronus, representing the Titans to castrate his father with a sickle which she provided.

Cronus performed this task, thus making heaven (Uranus) impotent and sterile. The dark blood from this act fell upon the land, and from this blood the Furies were born; some of the sperm fell into the sea and created a foam, and from this Aphrodite (Venus) was born, as the female creative principle born from heaven's loss.

Uranus is depicted as heaven or in some cases the heavenly man or creative will of god. Saturn/Cronus, the god of time and structure born of the union between Uranus and Gaia, took rule over the Earth (primal matter), which Uranus as the Creative Will had shaped into form and existence.

Uranus also represented an ancient celestial group and reigned over a spiritual race—before we descended into physical form. In Madame Blavatsky's *The Secret Doctrine*, we read:

> Thus while Uranus, or the Host representing this celestial group, reigned and ruled over the Second Race and their then Continent; Cronus or Saturn governed the Lemurians; and Jupiter, Neptune and others fought in the allegory for Atlantis, which was the whole Earth in the day of the Fourth Race. Poseidonis, or the last island of Atlantis . . . lasted till about 12,000 years ago.[3]

So we see from the above that the ancient mythical literature is descriptive of how the planetary rulers were depicted through the great world cycles. This descriptive mythology exists in all world cultures: the names are different but the stories are almost the same. In Egyptian mythology the female sky god called Nut lay with her twin brother, Geb the Earth. It is said that she did this against the wishes of her father, Ra, who had the couple brutally separated by Shu (the name derived from a verb which means to raise) who supports and separates the Earth from the Heavens. But Geb and Nut still managed to have five children; they were Osiris, his sister and wife Isis, Horus (also known as the son of Osiris and Isis as well as their brother), Set or Seth the evil brother, and his sister Nephthys who was also Set's wife—although within this last marriage there were no offspring.

[3] Madame Blavatsky, *The Secret Doctrine*, vol. 2, pp. 808, 809.

The myths attributed to Ra the Sun god show him as the first creator of men and living creatures (not physical creations), he brought into being a "new universe" which was different from the present world in which he resided. As Ra grew old, the ingratitude of these non-physical creations brought on a great distaste, then Nut (heaven) took Ra (the Sun) on her back and raised him right up into the heavens: at this time, it is said, our present world was created.

The God Anhur (Onouris, not Ouranus) also identified with Shu, means the "leader who has gone," (also translated as "sky bearer." Shu may somehow link in with Nut and Ra because he helped to raise up the creative power of the Sun and Heavens. However, the Romans linked Shu with Ares, god of war.

Uranus was said to be the first astronomical teacher, also called Jyotisha (one of the names of Brahma). In China the sky god, Tien (or Ouranus), was also known as the first teacher of astronomy. Blavatsky says that Diodorus speaks of Uranus as the first king of Atlantis, confusing the continents, but that Plato indirectly corrects this statement.

The tarot card associated with Uranus is the card that has no number, the card of the Fool, also known as Maat or The Joker. Few versions of the early tarot cards give any positive interpretation because The Joker did not fit into earthly existence. Some older tarot cards show The Fool as a rather silly looking man wearing a fool's cap, his clothes torn and a bundle over his shoulder; a dog is biting his leg. He is not looking where he is going and is about to fall over a precipice, where in some versions of the cards a crocodile waits to devour him.

In A. E. Waite's tarot deck (known as The Rider-Waite deck), although the illustration is kinder and he acknowledges the Fool's higher attributes, in a divinatory sense this card is still seen as negative whichever way it falls. He describes it as folly, mania, extravagance, intoxication, delirium and frenzy. And—reversed—as negligence, absence, distribution, carelessness, nullity and vanity. And yet he says when describing the card:

> His countenance is full of intelligence and expectant dream. He has a rose in one hand and in the other a costly wand, from which depends over his right shoulder a wallet curiously embroidered. He is a prince of the other world on his travels through this one—all amidst the morning glory, in the keen

air. The sun, which shines behind him, knows whence he came, whither he is going, and how he will return by another path after many days. He is the spirit in search of experience. Many symbols of the Instituted Mysteries are summarized in this card, which reverses, under high warrants, all the confusions that have preceded it.[4]

Frederic Lionel explains that the Fool depicts a transcendental reality, and that is possibly why so many people find this difficult to put into practice in the material world.

As a Joker in the everyday deck of cards, the Fool supplants all the others. Therefore he is outside the game, placed just as easily at the beginning as at the end. Illustrating a transcendental Reality—the Apha and Omega of manifestation—Maat or the Fool, can only be appreciated through symbols. A symbol veils that which appears not, while inciting one to perceive an essential thought in its enigmatic envelope.[5]

The Fool in Shakespeare's *King Lear* often appeared more wise than the King himself. He was truthful to the king and always had an answer to the king's questions, although, being a fool, he appeared guileless and naive; perhaps because of this the king listened to him. In one speech he said:

I marvel what kin thou and thy daughters are: they'll have me whipped for speaking true, thou'lt have him whipped for lying, and sometimes I am whipped for holding my peace. I had rather be any kind o' thing than a fool: and yet I would not be thee, nuncle; thou hast pared thy wit o' both sides, and left nothing i' the middle.[6]

---

[4]A. E. Waite, *The Pictorial Key to the Tarot* (York Beach, ME: Samuel Weiser, 1973), pp. 152, 155.

[5] Frederic Lionel, *The Magic Tarot* (London: Routledge & Kegan Paul, 1982), pp. 162, 163.

[6]William Shakespeare *King Lear* Act 1, Scene IV. From *Shakespeare Arranged for Modern Reading*, edited by Frank W. Cady and Van H. Cartmen (New York: Doubleday, 1969), p. 950.

Many with difficult placements or aspects to Uranus can appear foolish, or eccentric, or different in some way. With both the flowing and hard aspects there is always a strong will present and such people are not easily led. In fact, just the opposite, for they will often go out of their way to "be different" and dislike constraint in any form.

Long before the planet Uranus was discovered, its name was known within the creative arts as well as mythology. In the 15th century, the Muses—initiates of the harmony of the universe—speak of ". . . Urania, Astronomy, transports us from the body of the serpent altogether (the loop of whose tail suggests the sun door), to the very feet of the highest transformation of the Father, sheer light."[7]

The highest interpretation of Uranus and Neptune leads towards the evolution of consciousness and the development of inspiration, inner vision and enlightenment.[8]

[7] Joseph Campbell, *The Masks of God: Creative Mythology* (New York: Penquin, 1976).

[8] See *The Awakening of Kundalini* by Gopi Krishna (Bombay, India: D. B. Taraporevala Sons & Co., 1983), published under the auspices of the Kundalini Research Foundation.

# 13

# URANUS IN
# SIGN AND HOUSE

> Uranus energy often seeks freedom beyond all boundaries. But gen-
> uine freedom implies an equal amount of responsibility. In defer-
> ence to planetary protocol, Saturn precedes Uranus and will confer
> genuine freedom only after a person has accepted the responsibility
> ascribed to it. The polar opposite of responsibility is willfulness. In
> early life (even into the 40s), this may be expressed as a wanton or
> reckless drive for freedom with complete disregard for the rights
> of others. The pejorative side of Uranus seeks to avenge itself in a
> rebellious way, all in the guise of freedom. These individuals first
> need to recognize how they are expressing their drive for freedom.
> Then they should seek the meaning of true freedom and try to under-
> stand their previous concepts concerning it. Pure freedom is possi-
> ble only when we responsibly consider other people and
> situations.
>
> —Doris Hebel[1]

Uranus is the seventh planet from the Sun. It orbits the Sun every 84.01
years, spending an average period of seven years in each sign. Uranus was
thought to have five moons, but in 1986 the second of the Voyager Probes
found ten small moons in addition to the five visible by telescope from
Earth. The same probes also discovered that the ring system, originally
discovered in 1977, consists of eleven rings in all, the rings being char-
coal black, and possibly debris of former moonlets which had broken up.

---

[1] Doris Hebel, *Celestial Psychology* (Santa Fe, NM: Aurora Press, 1985) p. 45.

It is thought that Uranus has a large rocky core covered by ice; its atmosphere is mainly hydrogen and helium, with traces of methane which give the planet a greenish tint.

The spin axis of Uranus is tilted at 98 degrees (the Earth, Mars, Saturn, and Neptune are tilted toward the Sun at angles from 23 to 29 degrees) so that at times its poles are pointed toward the Sun, giving the planet Uranus extreme seasons. Due to this tilted axis, we on Earth may sometimes observe Uranus at its equator and at others its north pole.

The German born British astrologer, William Herschel (1738-1822) discovered Uranus in 1781. Herschel had been a professional musician who also instructed himself in mathematics and astronomy, constructing his own reflecting telescope. While searching the night sky for double stars, he saw something he had never before noticed, although it appeared cloudy, it did have a flat shape and a definite movement. He informed the Astrologer Royal about his discovery and soon many knew of this planet. Instant fame followed for Herschel, and in 1782, he became the private astronomer to George III. In his lifetime he cataloged over 800 double stars, and found over 2,500 nebulae, thus establishing the basic form of the Galaxy; this information was all chronicled by his sister, Caroline Herschel. After his death his work was continued by his son, John Herschel.

William Herschel was the first modern person to discover a planet: all the other planets were known before recorded history, and Uranus had been discovered because of the relatively new invention of the telescope.[2]

## URANUS IN SIGN AND HOUSE

Uranus is the planet of the inventor and innovator, the planet of change and sudden revelation. In your personal chart, Uranus will show where originality is needed in your life, and what new approach you can make to change. It will help you decide where you need to break away from the status quo, indicating areas where freedom, autonomy, liberty, and independence of spirit exist. Less positively it will also show you where you may be "flaky," unpredictable, changeable, self-willed and disruptive, also where you may experience disruption and sudden periodic changes.

---

[2] Invention of the refractor telescope (using lenses) is attributed to a Dutch optician, Hans Lippershay, in 1608. The first reflector telescope (using mirrors) was built in 1670 by Isaac Newton.

The sign Uranus falls in[3] will apply generally to all those born during the seven year period when Uranus occupies the sign. The house Uranus falls in will show the more personalized way that this influence will make itself felt within your individual personality. Aspects to Uranus in the natal chart should also be noted, particularly aspects to the Sun, Moon, Mercury, or Ascendant.

When reading Uranus in sign and house, also look to the house which is ruled or co-ruled by Uranus (the house with Aquarius on the cusp). This will be of less significance, but certainly should be noted.

## URANUS IN THE 1ST HOUSE
**(Uranus in Aries, 1928 to 1935)**

The 1st house is the house of personality, so with Uranus positioned here you will be out of the ordinary in some way, always seeking new and interesting ways to express your uniqueness. Your personality is certainly very lively and original, but whether this originality will be used constructively or not will be determined by other aspects to your chart.

If you have only good aspects to Uranus, you will be a trail blazer, discovering new and inventive ways to deal with your own and other's problems. Your comprehension will be quick and clear; you will not be satisfied to follow traditional rules imposed on you by society, but will strive for reforms as well as initiating new and inventive paths for others to follow. However, even with the good aspects, you will have a certain restless ambition and a certain difficulty in forming a stable personality.

With the difficult aspects, you rarely take others into your consideration, making your own rules as you go along. Eccentric and rebellious behavior can cause you to have a selfish attitude bent on getting your own way—with sheer disregard for other people's points of view. Because of your independent manner and lack of convention, you can make life difficult for others, often through antisocial behavior, and by regarding the point of view of others as totally irrelevant. The original side of your personality—when negative—is used only for your personal gain, with complete disregard for others' freedom or ideas. This type of behavior can make any partnership you have extremely difficult, and the disruptive

---

[3] For exact dates see tables on page 168.

behavior patterns generated by this placement often cause irretrievable breakdown within personal relationships.

Your chart will likely show both positive as well as hard aspects to Uranus, but even with the positive aspects, balance from Saturn is essential for grounding you, and helping you to understand the limitations, as well as the uniqueness, of your personality. The challenge you meet with Uranus in the 1st house revolves around the need to find your real self, rather than the superficial personality self within you. Uranus in your chart shows where change is needed, but if the need for change within your personality goes unheeded, then Uranus's sudden and disruptive element will force issues into your life which bring disruption and unpleasant situations which will work against you and your selfish and erratic tendencies.

## URANUS IN THE 2ND HOUSE
**(Uranus in Taurus, 1935 to 1942)**

The 2nd house is the house connected to your money and the money you earn, as well as your possessions, your inner values and resources (including your talents and gifts); the 2nd house is also representative of your inner security. Uranus in Taurus or the 2nd house suggests some changes may need to be made in some—if not all—of these areas.

With the difficult aspects or transits, you may resent the freedom that money brings to others, while refusing to accept change upon your own monetary pathway; change may then be forced on you, in the form of a sudden loss of earnings or loss of money through investments. The more negative aspects or transits will always cause some difficulties within the financial situation. Moneywise, you may experience sudden gain or loss, often with changes for the worse. Although you can sometimes take great care within your financial situation, you may also have a sudden need to spend money, which may precipitate a difficult financial problem. Likewise your feelings can be very liberal and generous, but also changeable and unstable at times.

Your attitudes over money were formed from early family influences, which usually developed through and in accordance with your family position as well as its financial status. Uranus in the 2nd house shows the need for a new approach to your money, your possessions and securities, as well as recognizing and developing talents and gifts which are representative of the 2nd house.

With the more positive aspects, money can be earned in an unusual way, such as through astrology or the occult, or some other new age technology that can also contain a scientific vein. Independence in issues connected to money is common. Well aspected, you may have an original way of giving to others. You always value freedom, and this position can often produce a possessiveness of your own independence, liberty, and space.

To free yourself from negative childhood programming in regard to your inner security and value systems, work to understand Saturn's influence upon your chart. For it is through recognizing where Saturn's restrictions, limitations and inferiorities cause over-reliance on material success and prosperity (or in some cases a turning away from wealth, as seen in those who reject family values, or disrupt things just for the sake of change) that you liberate the independent and creative spirit of Uranus to take you into a new and freer value-system based on new values and goals, leaving past fears and insecurities far behind.

## URANUS IN THE 3RD HOUSE
**(Uranus in Gemini, 1942 to 1949)**

The 3rd house represents the mind, communication, learning before high school, short journeys and siblings. Uranus in Gemini (or the 3rd house) may give you very original thought processes, sometimes not fully appreciated by others. Many may think your views odd, particularly if you have the more difficult aspects. However, the good aspects can bestow the brightest of minds with many original ideas, although even with the good aspects a certain flakiness of thinking and unpredictability in thought is common. Often you will find your mind is in the future, and your thoughts may even be several years ahead of popular social convention.

With both positive and negative aspects to Uranus your mind may be changeable, shifts in your thinking upsetting others as well as yourself. Your thoughts may be disorganized, erratic, quirky, although at other times your originality is remarkable if somewhat unconventional.

By working with and understanding the limitations and disciplines of Saturn in your chart, you begin to develop the discipline which is so badly needed to bring more focus to your mind, thus allowing the liveliness and vivacity of your imagination to facilitate new and inventive ways to look at—and work through—old problems, both personally and collectively. A more focused mind also allows you to develop your talents, and to implement your—now—more tangible ideas in a more practical way within yourself, society, and the world.

## URANUS IN THE 4TH HOUSE
### (Uranus in Cancer, 1949 to 1956)

The 4th house represents the home, the family, mother and mother figures, the emotions as developed through family interaction, your habitual responses to life. With Uranus in the 4th house there can be sudden changes in domestic or family life. You can be self-willed in connection to other family members, particularly your mother, for your emotions may not be talked out, with the consequences that you may have sudden emotional outbursts, or make sudden decisions that are emotionally based before even consulting others. Difficult circumstances may have affected your early childhood environment, with the consequence that you find it hard to ever feel secure. No matter how much you try to bring stability into your home life, something always seems to disrupt your security.

With Uranus in the 4th house an original approach is needed that allows you to work through the emotional turmoil you experienced when young, and which continues to generate many upsetting—but often unconscious—family memories. You may have witnessed a breakdown in relations between your parents, they may have been divorced, or due to other factors your family life may have suddenly been disrupted. Your father's career may have necessitated many changes of family residence, or you may have been placed in various homes or establishments away from the family (boarding schools, children's homes, or foster homes). Another way Uranus may manifest in the 4th house is that, in your childhood, your home life may have been very unconventional, or you may have experienced too much freedom with the consequence of tension developing whenever you try to settle down.

It is by investigating family memories related to childhood that you can begin to let go of the past. In order to do this, look to Saturn's placement within your chart, and work with the difficulties and restrictions this planet imposes on your human condition. Until you can do this, emotionally you will continue to be unsure of exactly what you want, who you want, as well as where you want to be.

## URANUS IN THE 5TH HOUSE
**(Uranus in Leo, 1956 to 1962)**

The 5th house is the house of love and love affairs, affection, enjoyment, pleasure, and it is the house of self-expression and creativity, the house of your children. If you have Uranus in the 5th house, love and creative enjoyment have to go hand in hand with freedom, although self-will and arrogance may sabotage many of your more personal endeavors, particularly those connected to affairs of the heart. When love, enjoyment or creative endeavor are denied (by yourself or others) you experience a degree of tension and unease which often causes you to develop erratic and intolerable behavior patterns, leading to a lack of sensitivity, which, in the case of love relationships, can only alienate you more from those you love. You can fall in or out of love in an instant, and love affairs may begin and end rather suddenly. Children can also be a source of tension with the hard aspects.

With the more positive aspects to Uranus in the 5th house, the Uranian influence may manifest within your life in a creative sense if, that is, you allow your Self the freedom to develop. The person you love may be brilliant or unusual in some way, or someone who does not follow the beaten track, or they may be from a foreign culture, or original in some other special way, or creative in connection to the stage or the arts.

To use your originality in service to the Self seems the obvious answer to Uranus in the 5th, but somehow this can be very difficult for you. Until specific lessons within the personality are understood and integrated, this position of Uranus can cause many problems because of a self-willed and antagonistic sense of self. In order to better understand your own personal uniqueness first work with the lessons of Saturn, understand the difference between the personality self and the Soul Self, if you can do this, you begin to find out that freedom to have your own way is only an illusion, and that freedom to be your Self is a completely different thing.

# URANUS IN THE 6TH HOUSE
## (Uranus in Virgo, 1962 to 1969)

The 6th house is the house of work and service to others, health and diet, it is also representative of those you employ. You will need to have freedom in your work: repetitive, commonplace tasks make if difficult for you to maintain interest in employment, bringing instability and frustration into your working environment. Your everyday life and domestic chores often prove to be irksome, boring and tedious, and your working patterns erratic. You will need to have as much freedom as possible within the area of your work, because you resent supervision and interference from others.

Positive aspects to this position may provide a very original mind when it comes to the health and well being of others. You may be an innovator finding many new—as well as resurrecting many old—healing alternatives to help mankind. You could have an interest in astrological techniques, using this in your work and service to others, including the help you give to family and friends. On the other hand you may work in the more technical sphere, with computers or other modern technology, or you may find some other scientific, or even astronomical employment. Those you employ will sometimes be of a Uranian type (often born under Aquarius), and faddyness in diet is common.

With Uranus in the 6th house, highly strung nerves are often experienced, and your health may sometimes be impaired because of a highly strung nervous system—even with the positive aspects. Uranus in the 6th house can also in some instances denote attunement to a higher consciousness, due to the physical structure's greater sensitivity to higher vibrationary levels. With both positive and hard aspects strange aches, pains and ailments may suddenly occur; these, however, may often be eradicated by an unorthodox approach, and complementary medicine.

In order to bring out the inventiveness of Uranus in the 6th house, first investigate Saturn's position on your chart. Work to understand the restrictive principle symbolized by Saturn that is inherent within your life and start to turn it around to a strength rather than a weakness. If you can begin to do this, the higher message from Uranus will start to become apparent, and will be reflected back in the freedom your work and service gives to others, as well as the freedom your work will ultimately give to you.

# URANUS IN THE 7TH HOUSE
## (Uranus in Libra, 1969 to 1975)

The 7th house represents one to one relationships and partnerships, the spouse, the shadow[4], and in traditional astrology was also representative of open enemies. With Uranus in the 7th house you will be attracted to unconventional partners, and unusual relationships may be sought. The more positive aspects imply that any difficulty within marriage or partnerships can be worked through in an original way. One astrologer suggested that partnering an astrologer or a person with Universal views would be one way to use Uranus in the 7th house.

With the more difficult aspects to Uranus, sudden changes in your relationships may occur (although other more positively placed planets in the 7th house may nullify some of the more difficult aspects to Uranus). You may experience sudden affairs, and divorces, instigated by you or the other person. You may have a sudden breakup of close relationships, and intolerable tensions developing between you and your partner. You may also experience an uncomfortable and jittery feeling in the presence of certain people.

Difficult aspects to Uranus in the 7th house keep you locked into upsetting and intolerable relationship problems, while the more positive aspects allow you much greater freedom within relationships than you could ever imagine. Try to understand the reason for Saturn's restrictive influence within your life. When you can do this, Uranus in the 7th house can lead you to a new understanding of relationships, so that within all the restrictions that partnerships bring, you experience a true freedom, instead of always wanting to be free or to stand alone. If you can follow your independent path—within the confines or your moral obligations—while at the same time allowing your partner to follow theirs, then you will find the sort of freedom you have always sought but never found, but this can only be won through first recognizing the confines and structures of Saturn.

---

[4] *The Saturn/Pluto Phenomenon*, p. 38.

# URANUS IN THE 8TH HOUSE
**(Uranus in Scorpio, 1975 to 1981)**

The 8th house represents all shared resources with others, such as those found in deep emotional and sexual involvements, it also represents others' money and so is connected to tax and inheritance. The 8th house is the house of death, rebirth, and transformation, also representing in-depth psychology. It is the house of the arcane and occult.

With the positive aspects would come a natural understanding of esoteric, or hidden pathways. Originality may also occur in regard to other people's money and values. The positive aspects may bestow upon you a certain sexual attractiveness, and may even help you to develop new and unusual ways of dealing with deep psychological problems—yours and other people's. With the more difficult aspects to Uranus in the 8th house, you may seek some excitement through sexual pleasures. Unusual sexual practices may occur, or a fear of you or your partner not being quite normal in your sexual appetites may manifest, although this is not always the case. Often a certain sexual excitement is required in some form, and sudden sexual relationships of short duration may be common.

As the 8th house also involves others' money and values, as well as shared resources with others, the difficult aspects imply there may be a sudden loss in this area. This may be the loss of a sexual or emotional relationship, or a business venture may founder and joint finances may be lost. There could be a sudden and heavy tax demand, or sudden loss or even gain of an inheritance. The suddenness of these occurrences will throw you back upon yourself, teaching you that nothing lasts, and that everything is transitory.

Difficult aspects to Uranus will keep you tied to past irrationalities, while the more positive aspects allow you more freedom to develop an entirely new perspective on many past problems. To fully utilize this position of Uranus, first look to Saturn's placement within your chart; work to understand the restrictions and structures of your own existence, then the many blessings from Uranus may start to illuminate the transforming darkness of this 8th house placement.

# URANUS IN THE 9TH HOUSE
**(Uranus in Sagittarius, 1981 to 1988)**

The 9th house is the house of higher learning, wisdom, law, and morality. The 9th house also represents colleges and universities, esoteric religion, long journeys (both of the mind and body), and foreign travel. These journeys abroad will often greatly change and expand the mind.

Philosophy, higher learning in any form—including the scientific— is well marked here, even with some of the more difficult aspects. If Uranus is favorably aspected, a great deal of learning of a higher nature is done in this life. The mind is usually very original, unprejudiced, bright, open, and astute. This is one of the best placements for Uranus and much good can be derived from it. Uranus in the 9th house is leading to a revolution in your views, with much questioning of the status quo.

Your thinking may be ahead of its time, and others with more mundane thought processes often will not recognize or understand yours; even with the good aspects, this can lead to a certain loneliness at times. Other difficulties from negative aspects to Uranus in the 9th house would perhaps include, sudden changes within academic life, and the mind being so "flaky" that it never really stays with a subject long enough to understand it thoroughly.

The more difficult aspects to Saturn may block you developing Uranus's more progressive qualities into a purer form of awareness. If this is the case, look to Saturn's position within your chart. Work to understand *why* the reason for the pain and limitations of this world, as well as why the necessary lessons must be learned from Saturn. Then use this knowledge in order to release your Higher Mind to soar toward a truth and wisdom beyond all earthly restrictions and material concerns.

# URANUS IN THE 10TH HOUSE
**(Uranus in Capricorn, 1988 to 1996)**

The 10th house represents the world, the career, authority figures—which traditionally include the father—and your place in society. With Uranus in this house you often find originality in your career, and unusual and interesting ways of presenting yourself—and sometimes others—to the world, as in advertising and publicity where original features capture the public's notice. Scientific work, particularly with computers, may also be a congenial profession. This position of Uranus can also produce the true humanitarian or philanthropist.

With Uranus in the 10th house, you need a career that also allows you a great deal of freedom, having little tolerance for authority, and usually preferring to be your own boss. Throughout your life you may make sudden career changes, and you usually have no hesitation in throwing over an old and secure career that seems no longer attractive, in order to make way for a business move in a new and more interesting direction.

Easy aspects to Uranus cause the above to be achieved with ease, but the more difficult aspects may cause you to have sudden difficult or upsetting career changes, difficulty in getting on with authority figures, or a self-willed and contrary stance to the world in general—all due to an intolerable tension that often arises within you. Often this tension will cause you to throw over a secure position simply for the sake of change, although in some cases other parts of your personality, which require more security, will force you to hold onto a career that is not a true expression of your real needs and goals.

Uranus in the 10th house can, in some instances, cause quite a radical disposition to develop regarding the world and society. In order to allow Uranus's true uniqueness and sense of brotherhood to develop within the world, first look to the position of Saturn in your chart. Work to understand the reason for some of the restrictions and frustrations within your life. Saturn rules Capricorn and the 10th house, and it is by recognizing the needs of your life, as well as the reasons for its structures, that the message of Uranus is made clear to you.

# URANUS IN THE 11TH HOUSE
## (Uranus in Aquarius, 1996 to 2003)

The 11th house is the house of friends, groups, associations, as well as aspirations and ideals. The 11th house is the house of Aquarius, and Uranus is now its accepted ruler, so Uranus is at home here. Unusual and unique friends are common with this placement, and friendships are often based on humanitarian and universal causes.

With Uranus in the 11th house, friends and groups can prove lively, stimulating, and original. Positive aspects suggest that much good can come from this placement, and group involvement will draw you toward social ideals and idealistic philosophies, and many close friendships can be made through group activities. As the 11th house is also the house connected to ideals and aspirations, intuitive comprehension often flows through you into both personal and group consciousness, allowing humanity's evolutionary intentions to be made manifest.

With the more difficult aspects, you may choose friends whose attitudes are rather too radical and extremist at times, or there may be sudden breaks in friendships. But always you will be drawn to people who are unusual and innovative in some way. Sometimes you or your acquaintances may develop such overly detached attitudes that no real friendships ever come about, or your urge for freedom within friendships and group activities can cause you to be so highly individualistic that problems will inevitably arise. Occasionally with Uranus in the 11th house your ideals within friendships and groups can become so utopian that you hardly ever find any individual—or any group—that comes up to your high aspirations.

To truly develop the aspirations and ideals on Earth of Uranus and the 11th house, first look to Saturn's placement within your chart, for without structure and form within your life, no true aspirations may ever be achieved. For only when you understand some of Saturn's message will you also begin to learn the reason for, as well as the true meaning of, Uranus' universal aims.

## URANUS IN THE 12TH HOUSE
**(Uranus in Pisces, 2003 to 2011)**

The 12th house is the house of confinement and sacrifice, also the house of the unconscious mind. Strong intuitive flashes of genius may spring from the unconscious or, on the other hand (with the more difficult aspects) sudden self-willed obstinacy may be derived from a hidden, unconscious impulse.

The 12th house can contain unconscious motivations and memories, as well as repressed and forgotten experiences—some of which may be quite painful. Uranus in this house may suddenly trigger off certain repressed childhood memories and traumas, which can then be projected onto people and events in your immediate world, often causing misery and misunderstandings within many important relationships. By recognizing the motivation derived from unconscious memories, you can begin to release yourself from the past, as well as learning to stop blaming those around you for how you feel.

Difficult aspects to Uranus keep you tied to past and unconscious pain, while more positive aspects allow sudden insight and release from the anguish caused by unconscious mental injury. In order to release some of these distressing unconscious blocks, first work to understand the impact of both Uranus and Saturn within your chart.

Once you understand exactly what the restrictions from Saturn imply within your life, as well as why you have the need to keep fighting them, you will stop blaming those around you for your present difficulties, and the intuitive flashes of genius from Uranus in the 12th house will begin to permeate the dark corners of past misunderstandings and fears that still lurk within your—as yet—unenlightened unconscious. When you can begin finally to acknowledge and let go of all the hurt you feel, you release an energy that can be directed into far more productive and creative channels.

# 14

# URANUS

> You shall be free indeed when your days are not without a care nor your nights without a want and a grief.
>
> But rather when these things girdle your life and yet you rise above them naked and unbound.
>
> And how shall you rise above your days and your nights unless you break the chains which you at the dawn of your understanding have fastened around your noon hour?
>
> In truth that which you call freedom is the strongest of these chains, though its links glitter in the sun and dazzle your eyes.
>
> —Kahlil Gibran[1]

The deeper meaning of the freedom exemplified by Uranus is often hard to explain or understand; the poet Kahlil Gibran speaks of freedom as being the strongest chain that binds us—but only because we do not realize its true significance. So what is freedom's true significance, and where does Uranus come into the equation?

Transits or progressions to or from Uranus can often result in undefined and chaotic jumps into something new, caused mainly by the need for freedom in some area. Some release may be badly needed, but when the release is only of a material nature, often no lasting benefit is experienced; for real changes in personal freedom (as symbolized by Uranus' higher attributes) may only occur through a shift in awareness.

---

[1] Kahlil Gibran, *The Prophet* (New York: Alfred A. Knopf, 1975), pp. 51-52.

Your chart placement for Uranus will show where this freedom is needed, but liberation can only be won after we rise above the material side of life with all its worries and griefs. To do this we have to know ourselves on many different levels, so our thinking is not based on purely unconscious desires. This cannot be achieved through suppressing the lower nature in any way—in fact, just the opposite—it is done through understanding, loving and working with the human part of ourselves.

If we again look at the myth of Uranus, we see that after he coupled with Gaia, and a new god (Cronus) was born, man took on physical form[2] and sank into material existence: Cronus the god of time and structure—otherwise known as Saturn—took rule. Uranus (the creative or heavenly will) was no longer needed, and so was castrated by his son, Saturn: the blood from the wound fell onto land (the material) and from this contact the Furies were born. The word "fury" is described in the Oxford Dictionary as meaning fierce passion; wild anger; in a fit of rage; with great force or effort; the avenging spirit. This was our human heritage and thus became part of our nature.

But as Uranus' blood fell upon land, so the sperm from the wounded genitals fell into the sea (the unconscious, the infinite and divine wisdom). From this foam was born Aphrodite (Venus): the female creative principle born of the seed from heaven. And so humankind, through this heavenly element, was also given the power to create and was endowed with inventive imagination and imaginative thought. God had created man and woman, and when they were able to rise above the Furies, they were also given the same ability as god to create. Howard Sasportas in his book *The Gods of Change*, says:

> This part of the myth suggests that Venus—the principle of love, beauty, harmony, diplomacy and balance—can be born from the tension between Saturnian forces of homoeostasis and Uranian forces of disruption and change. The birth of Venus indicates the possibility of presenting new ideas and alternatives in a way that is tactful and diplomatic, and will not be so threatening to the existing order of things.[3]

---

[2] See page 97. Uranus in Myth, Legend and Literature.

[3] Howard Sasportas, *The Gods of Change* (London: Arkana, 1989), p.37.

But a human ruled by the Furies often experienced, instead, violent passion and greed, anger and jealousy, and only occasionally did he think he could hear some other voice. Besides when sunk so deep into corporeal life he could not be sure—and, anyway, anyone who hears voices is thought of as being a little mad.

Even before the knowledge of the planet Uranus (discovered in 1781 by William Herschel) some people of genius were subject to its force. Astrologers and those familiar with arcane knowledge were usually under the guidance of this higher Mercury. But the wisdom of the past also recognized the terrible destructive principle of this agent and often looked upon it more as an element of evil—for the Furies were so deep-seated and had such power that people rarely had any choice but to obey their obsessional demands.

How many of us accept change positively and use the Uranus energy to release ourselves from our self-imposed prisons, working inwardly with the archetypal images which really produce the restrictive principles upon which our life is built? Many of us do not bother to look within; instead we try to escape the status quo by dramatically changing our life style and habits. But often this is no different from changing our clothes—we are still essentially the same underneath.

Uranus in good aspect to personal planets produces a revolutionary and reforming spirit, a progressive mind and much originality—which can be used both personally and collectively. Added to this is a strong intuition, a flexible intellect, and often the ability to influence other people.

Uranus in difficult aspect causes self-will, obstinacy and a contradictory nature, plus various states of tension which lead to setbacks and other upsetting circumstances. There is a tendency to have "too many irons in the fire," often coupled with over-estimation of self, nervousness and eccentric actions, and with much "flakiness" of mind and intention.

Often both positive and negative elements will work together, although the degree to which they do so is determined by other chart factors, including the shadow aspect[4] as illuminated by Saturn's placement. Stephen Arroyo points out how Uranus' positive and negative elements interweave.

> In considering aspects with Uranus, as with the aspects of the other trans-Saturnian planets, it is misleading to evaluate a particular configuration as *a priori* likely to be expressed

---

[4] See pages 38-39, *The Saturn/Pluto Phenomenon*.

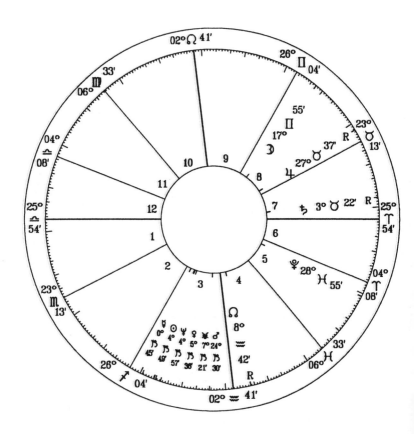

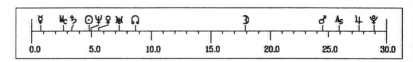

*Chart 10. Louis Pasteur's chart. December 27, 1822, 2:00 A.M. GMT. Dole, Jura, France. Placidus houses. Data from* The American Book of Charts. *Chart calculated by Astrolabe using* Nova Printwheels.

constructively or destructively; for, more than any other planet, Uranus represents the level of consciousness where one thinks and acts in a *both/and* way rather than in an *either/or* fashion. In other words, a Uranian person usually expresses some of both polarities: positive *and* negative; and he may express both simultaneously.[5]

If we remember that Uranus is the Higher Mercury, then we see that the Uranus placement, like Mercury's, is dependent on other factors within the natal chart, and a thorough investigation of the chart is necessary to access on the level on which Uranus is likely to operate.

Louis Pasteur (1822-1895), the French microbiologist, has a conjunction of the Sun and Uranus (See Chart 10) as has Saddam Hussein of Iraq (Chart 11 on page 122).

Pasteur's chart shows the Sun in Capricorn conjunct Uranus-Venus-Neptune and Mercury in the 3rd house, all trine Saturn in Taurus in the 7th house, suggesting this conjunction was used for the benefit of others. The conjunction between the Sun-Uranus-Venus-Neptune and Mercury were all square to Pluto in the 5th house.

In Saddam's chart the Sun's aspects are an inconjunct to the Moon, as well as a conjunction with Uranus in Taurus in the 8th house, although interestingly enough Uranus trines Neptune, Neptune in turn trines Mercury and bi-quintiles Venus. The Moon, however, conjuncts Mars, inconjuncts Uranus, and squares Neptune. Although Saturn is well-aspected by planet, it is in its fall in Aries, and opposes the Ascendant and squares the Midheaven (both the later aspects are also found in Pasteur's chart). A t-square is formed by Venus on the cusp of the 8th house, Jupiter in the 5th, and Pluto on the cusp of the 11th house.

If we look at Uranus through some case histories, we may understand better the essence of this planet's influence. Gerald was a very lively person who liked to follow new age trends in thinking. In one way this was very productive, as he was inventive and original in his chosen career. However, his personal life was very different: he had Uranus in the 1st house trine Mercury and Venus in the 10th. His original character, when not being harnessed productively in his career, became very willful and

---

[5] Stephen Arroyo, *Astrology, Karma & Transformation* (Sebastapol, CA:CRCS Publications, 1978), p. 116.

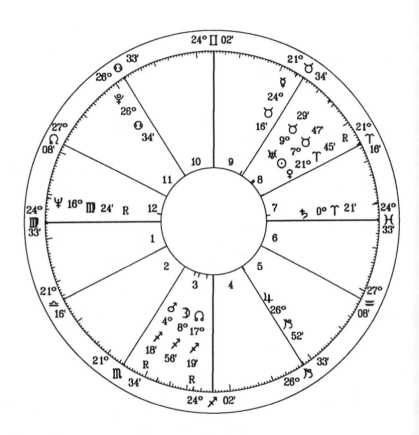

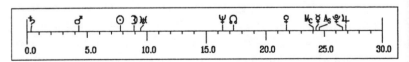

*Chart 11. Saddam Hussein's chart. April 28, 1937, 12:15 P.M. GMT. 34:36 N; 43:42 E. Placidus houses. Chart calculated by Astrolabe using Nova Printwheels. Data from the Astrology Trading Centre, London.*

self-seeking in his more personal relationships. He seemed to be set on getting his own way within relationships, enhancing his own romantic and emotional needs. See Chart 12, page 124.

Gerald's chart shows Neptune in Libra in the 5th, which squares Uranus in the 1st and the North Node in the 8th. Note also Saturn's painful position in Scorpio in the 5th. This all came to a head when he became very friendly with one of his clients who confided her marital problems to him. He persuaded her that her marriage was in a rut, and that what she needed was to experience other relationships so that she could grow as a person. Rachel, with help from Gerald, left her husband of eighteen years and her five children and moved in with Gerald and his wife. Over the next few months Gerald had an affair with Rachel which finally came to a head when Rachel found another boyfriend and broke up the threesome.

Gerald took it badly that all his new age thoughts counted for nothing, as he experienced an overwhelming possessiveness and rage at her rejection. The point is that he enjoyed doing things that broke down other people's barriers of convention, but, when tested on a personal level in his turn, he was unable to cope emotionally.

If we took another chart with difficult aspects to Uranus, we can begin to understand its rather changeable and self-willed nature. Angela came for therapy to lose weight. She was 31 and had been happily married for three years. She explained how she thought she never would get married due to the fact she loved her freedom, but meeting the right man had changed everything. They had a beautiful apartment, good careers and everything was wonderful. Angela lost the required weight and then asked me to do her birth chart. See Chart 13 on page 126.

The main focus of Angela's chart was a t-square. She had Uranus in Cancer on the 8th house cusp square the Sun and Venus in Aries in the 4th, which opposed a Saturn-Neptune conjunction in Libra in the 10th house. I explained to her that when Uranus was triggered off by transit or progression there might be some disruptive element within her sexual relationships, but pointed out that she had freewill and could work with it if she chose. Her chart showed that in approximately a year's time the progressed Moon would conjunct Uranus in the 8th house, and I suggested she might like to come and work with it nearer to the time. She came for an appointment a year later as she said she felt "something" was happening.

As the progressed Moon formed a conjunction with Uranus in the 8th house, Angela suddenly felt very attractive and attracted by the opposite

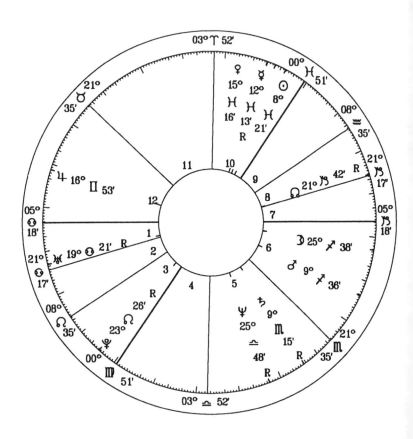

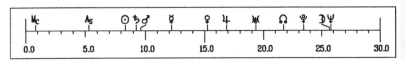

*Chart 12. Gerald's chart. Birth data from family has been withheld for confidentiality. Placidus houses. Chart calculated by Astrolabe using Nova Printwheels.*

sex. Three men were showing a great interest in her and she was really enjoying the attention. I suggested care was needed and perhaps she would like to investigate and work with how she was feeling. She wanted to know more about her chart and what the implications were of her having a new relationship; and *no,* she did not want to work with it. Three months later, her husband telephoned to say she had left him for a 17-year-old from a different culture, who was still at college.

Obviously Uranus in the 8th house in Angela's chart was experienced as freedom within the sexual experience, breaking taboos, having an unusual lover. Now this sounds fine, but a clearer look is required to see why she could not experience this within her original relationship. The Sun and Venus in Aries in the 4th house suggested her home and family were important to her, also she would need to feel she came first emotionally; but, as the Sun and Venus were opposing a Saturn-Neptune conjunction, this would have seriously undermined Angela's confidence in herself. Deep down she would feel that others were better than her. There was also a lack of self-worth—particularly within relationships—and regarding herself as a woman, from the painful Venus-Saturn opposition. Her romantic illusions concerning the lover only deluded her still further, as it probably did temporarily help her lack of self-esteem to feel desirable through his sexual passion. But the experience did nothing to give her lasting self-reliance or confidence within herself. Angela lost her home, was alienated from her family, and eventually found herself alone and very unhappy.

The higher interpretation of Uranus in Cancer in the 8th could be expressed as insight into her own emotions, personality, and sexuality as found in depth psychology or astrology. Any transformational analysis of her own nature could provide her with valuable insights as to her real needs. Pluto, the ruler of the 8th house and planet of transformation and rebirth, was in his own house squared Mars in 5th and Jupiter 6th, but was in positive aspect to every planet within the opposition, so this transforming energy may possibly come into play later in life as Angela works through further problems.

So, is Uranus in hard aspect and affected by difficult transits inevitably going to cause some major breakdown? I think the answer has to be, yes, unless the person concerned has learned to work with and understand his or her psyche to some degree. Angela's Sun[6] afflicted by Saturn and

---

[6] See *The Saturn/Pluto Phenomenon*, pp. 94-96.

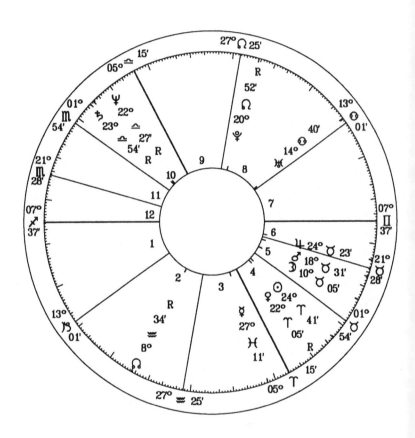

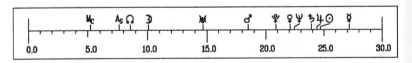

*Chart 13. Angela's chart. Birth data from family has been withheld for confidentiality. Placidus houses. Chart calculated by Astrolabe using* Nova Printwheels.

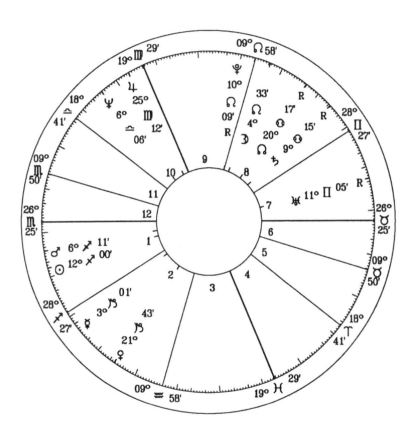

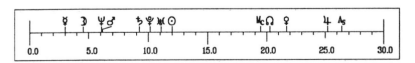

*Chart 14. Sarah's chart. Birth data from family has been withheld for confidentiality. Placidus houses. Chart calculated by Astrolabe using* Nova Printwheels.

Neptune showed she had little sense of Self, her lower ego was in charge, and so she had little choice in the final outcome. Although conscious choice had been offered her before the emotional upheaval occurred, when the progressed Moon conjuncted Uranus, she seemed completely unable to detach from her unconscious desire nature, and thus no real choice was ever made.

Another chart shows a similar pattern. Sarah (Chart 14, page 127) has Uranus in Gemini in the 7th house afflicted by the Sun and Mars in Sagittarius in the 1st, although the Sun is in good aspect to the Moon, Neptune, and Pluto. Sarah only comes for a therapy session when she is having problems within relationships. She has been married three times, and has also had a succession of live-in boyfriends. She always seems to have conflict within her personal relationships. Is this inevitable? Must all of her relationships go wrong? The answer has to be, yes, until she investigates the parts of her chart that so undermine her. Sarah's Saturn is in Cancer in the 8th house—in opposition to Mercury in the 2nd—showing deep-set emotional problems, particularly those connected to sexual issues, which she has great difficulty in discussing. Until she recognizes this part of herself, Uranus will work in a destructive way, for without insight into her own nature, she has no ability to detach from the lower ego, especially when challenged by the Uranus energy and its need for change. By not recognizing the pain caused by her inner needs, she is hanging on to outmoded complexes from her past, and is therefore a prisoner of herself. It is only through knowing herself that she may become free.

# 15

# URANUS AND THE
# REALM OF ARCHETYPAL IMAGES

> The children of the gods (that's us) are buried in darkness until the passage of time (evolution) can bring their consciousness out into the light. The life force is, needless to say, very potent. Man is much more afraid of the Light than he is of the Dark and will always shield his eyes against a truth which is brought to him prematurely. He will throw stones at it or even crucify it in order to remain in the comfortable shadow of his ignorance. But that is human nature and Man must not be condemned for his unconsciousness. He can and does condemn himself for the *conscious* use of the dark forces within him.
>
> —Alan Oken[1]

Uranus is a transpersonal planet — the Higher Mercury, therefore it is necessary to understand its influence on as many levels as possible. One very important factor with Uranus is the ability to bring about a symbolic understanding of the manifestation of the archetypal images.[2] Could you conceive of a world made up entirely of archetypal images? For it is these that produce our reality (actuality), and to change our reality we need to understand the influences which come via the planetary channels. Unless this can be achieved to some degree, the archetypes remain subliminal forces which govern all our unconscious motivations.

---

[1] Alan Oken, *As Above, So Below* in *Alan Oken's Complete Astrology* (New York: Bantam, 1980), p. 217.
[2] See *The Saturn/Pluto Phenomenon*, pp. 31, 32.

Even our thoughts are predestined.[3] This is because the planetary energies project images within our unconscious mind, images which form our conscious perception. (Perhaps "conscious" may not be quite the right word for a motivation and drive of which we are often entirely unaware.)

When a child is born, the dormant seeds of the personality lie within. As the child grows, so these seeds come to life within the psyche (meaning mind and emotions) in the form of needs, complexes, and desires. It is this archetypal symbolism which forms the child's reality (actuality) and whatever is experienced in physical life can only be felt through those energies which form conscious awareness.

No two persons ever see the same reality, because each is viewing life through his or her unconscious symbolism. To try to achieve the same satisfaction, talent, or happiness that we think we see others experiencing is an impossibility, for we all have differing inner worlds made up of different images producing thought patterns quite unique to ourselves.

Uranus in astrology is connected with changes, and one thing is certain: everything changes, nothing remains the same except for Absolute Truth, which is unchangeable. Yet, as Plato and Socrates recognized, to come nearer to that Truth requires a great deal of change from us, and our human principles and condition. They believed that Truth could not be found through formulas, or points of reference, or even mathematical rules showing the regularity of astrological bodies, but they realized that from such knowledge we do gain some insights into that very Truth which we seek.

The following text reveals much, and rather than summarize it, I prefer to let Plato's words speak for themselves. In the text Socrates is explaining to Glaucon, Adeimantus, and some other listeners how most people view the world and their reality.

> Now then, I proceeded to say, go on to compare our natural condition, so far as education and ignorance are concerned, to a state of things like the following. Imagine a number of men living in an underground cavernous chamber, with an entrance open to the light, extending along the entire length of the cavern, in which they have been confined, from their childhood, with their legs and necks so shackled, that they are obliged to sit still and look straight forwards, because their chains render it

---

[3] See page 140.

impossible for them to turn their heads round: and imagine a bright fire burning some way off, above and behind them, and an elevated roadway passing between the fire and the prisoners, with a low wall built along it, like the screens which conjurers put up in the front of their audience, and above which they exhibit their wonders.

I have it, he replied.

Also figure to yourself a number of persons walking behind this wall, and carrying with them statues of men, and images of other animals, wrought in wood and stone and all kinds of materials, together with various other articles, which overtop the wall; and, as you might expect, let some of the passers-by be talking, and others silent.

You are describing a strange scene, and strange prisoners.

They resemble us, I replied. For let me ask you, in the first place, whether persons so confined could have seen anything of themselves or of each other, beyond the shadows thrown by the fire upon the part of the cavern facing them?

Certainly not, if you suppose them to have been compelled all their lifetime to keep their heads unmoved.

And is not their knowledge of the things carried past them equally limited?

Unquestionably it is.

And if they were able to converse with one another, do you not think that they would be in the habit of giving names to the objects which they saw before them?

Doubtless they would.

Again: if their prison house returned an echo from the part facing them, whenever one of the passers-by opened his lips, to what, let me ask, could they refer the voice, if not to the shadow which was passing?

Unquestionably they would refer it to that.

Then surely such persons would hold the shadows of those manufactured articles to be the only realities.

Without a doubt they would.

Now consider what would happen if the course of nature brought them a relief from their fetters, and a remedy for their foolishness, in the following manner. Let us suppose that one of them has been released, and compelled suddenly to stand up, and turn his neck round and walk with open eyes towards the light; and let us suppose that he goes through all these actions with pain, and that the dazzling splendour renders him incapable of discerning those objects of which he used formerly to see the shadows. What answer would you expect him to make, if someone were to tell him that in those days he was watching foolish phantoms, but that now he is somewhat nearer to reality, and is turning to things more real, and sees more correctly; above all, if he were to point out to him the several objects that are passing by, and question him, and compel him to answer what they are? Should you not expect him to be puzzled, and to regard his old visions as truer than the objects now forced upon his notice?

Yes, much truer.

And if he were further compelled to gaze at the light itself, would not his eyes, think you, be distressed, and would he not shrink and turn away to the things which he could see distinctly, and consider them to be really clearer than the things pointed out to him?

Just so.

And if someone were to drag him violently up the rough and steep ascent from the cavern, and refuse to let him go till he had drawn him out into the light of the sun, would he not, think you, be vexed and indignant at such treatment, and on reaching the light, would he not find his eyes so dazzled by the glare as to

THE URANUS-NEPTUNE INFLUENCE / 133

be incapable of making out so much as one of the objects that are now called true?

Yes, he would find it so at first.

Hence, I suppose, habit would be necessary to enable him to perceive objects in the upper world. At first he will be most successful in distinguishing shadows; then he will discern the reflections of men and other things in water, and afterwards the realities; and after this he will raise his eyes to encounter the moon and stars, finding it less difficult to study the heavenly bodies and the heaven itself by night, than the sun and the sun's light by day.

Doubtless.

Last of all, I imagine, he will be able to observe and contemplate the nature of the sun, not as it appears in water or on alien ground, but as it is in itself in its own territory.

Of course.

His next step will be to draw the conclusions, that the sun is the author of the seasons and the years, and the guardian of all things in the visible world, and in a manner the cause of all those things which he and his companions used to see.

Obviously, this will be his next step.

What then? When he recalls to mind his first habitation, and the wisdom of the place, and his old fellow-prisoners, do you not think he will congratulate himself on the change, and pity them.

Assuredly he will.

And if it was their practice in those days to receive honour and commendation one from another, and to give prizes to him who had the keenest eye for a passing object, and remembered best all that used to precede and follow and accompany it, and from these data divined most ably what was going to come next, do you fancy that he will covet these prizes, and envy

those who receive honour and exercise authority among them?
Do you not rather imagine that he will feel what Homer
describes, and wish extremely

> "To drudge on the lands of a master
> Under a portionless wing."

and be ready to go through anything, rather than entertain those
opinions, and live in that fashion?

For my own part, he replied, I am quite of that opinion. I
believe he would consent to go through anything rather than
live that way.

And now consider what would happen if such a man were to
descend again and seat himself on his old seat? Coming so suddenly out of the sun, would he not find his eyes blinded by the
gloom of the place.

Certainly, he would.

And if he were forced to deliver his opinions again, touching the
shadows aforesaid, and to deliver the lists against those who
have always been prisoners, while his sight continued to dim,
and his eyes unsteady—and if this process of initiation lasted a
considerable time—would he not be made a laughing stock,
and would it not be said of him, that he had gone up only to
come back again with his eyesight destroyed, and that it was
not worth while even to attempt the ascent? And if any one
endeavoured to set them free and carry them to the light, would
they not go so far as to put him to death, if they could only
manage to get him into their power?

Yes, that they would.

Now this imaginary case, my dear Glaucon, you must apply in
all its parts to our former statements, by comparing the region
which the eye reveals, to the prison-house, and the light of the
fire therein to the power of the sun: and if, by the upward
ascent and the contemplation of the upper world, you understand the mounting of the soul into the intellectual region, you
will hit the tendency of my own surmises, since you desire to be

told what they are; though, God only knows whether they are correct. But, be that as it may, the view which I take of the subject is to the following effect. In the world of knowledge, the essential Form of Good is the limit of our inquiries, and can barely be perceived; but, when perceived, we cannot help concluding that it is in every case the source of all that is bright and beautiful—in the visible world giving birth to light and its master, and in the intellectual world dispensing, immediately and with full authority, truth and reason—and that whoever would act wisely, either in private or public, must set this Form of Good before his eyes.

. . . Our present argument shews us that there is a faculty residing in the soul of each person, and an instrument enabling each of us to learn; and that, just as we might suppose it to be impossible to turn the eye round from darkness to light without turning the whole body, so must this faculty, or this instrument, be wheeled round, in company with the entire soul, from the perishing world, until it be enabled to endure the contemplation of the real world and the brightest part thereof, which, according to us, is the Form of Good. Am I not right?[4]

The symbolism in Plato's *Republic* conveys some of his own perception of Truth, and reveals the illusion of the human condition which is buried in darkness and sees only shadows. The Uranus influence can help free us to look beyond the images and shadows, we can work and learn through Uranus—the Awakener—who can show us a new consciousness, where creative choice impels us from Plato's cave out into the sunlight of a new tomorrow, and a reality much nearer to Truth than anything we have hitherto experienced.

---

[4] *The Republic of Plato* Book VII, Translated into English by John Llewelyn Davies and David James Vaughan (London: MacMillan and Co., 1897), pp. 235-238, 240.

# 16

# URANUS—
# BRINGER OF CHANGE

In the Chinese view, all things and phenomena around us arise out of the patterns of change and are represented by the various lines of the trigrams and hexagrams.

—Fritjof Capra[1]

If the Uranus energy symbolizes the *creative will of god,* this can link in with the above statement that all phenomena come from, and out of, patterns of change. Uranus is the planet of change, and in a positive sense also represents unity—true freedom for all—brotherhood—recognition of our own special place in the universe. But put some of these universal ideas and principles into the mind of humans unable to detach from their own desire nature and it is easy to see that difficulties will arise. For these *universal ideas* cannot work productively until linked with a nature that has at least some detachment and understanding of its own human desires and limitations. Uranus can give the ability to understand the real meaning of freedom, but this *freedom* can only be realized by first accepting Saturn's message. The role of Saturn cannot be emphasized enough for, until Saturn is understood better, no progress can begin. We have to learn to develop flexibility within the necessity for structure and form in our own life.

If we deny the need for change, a transit—usually a hard aspect from Uranus—will severely shake the rigid structures of our life that we have tried so hard to build. Uranus' true message is *change,* but this *change* needs to be within our habitual thought patterns, and should involve the reconstruction of our own way of looking at the universe. It takes a great act of

---

[1] Fritjof Capra, *The Tao of Physics* (New York: Bantam, 1977), p. 272.

*Those with Uranus prominent can change themselves as well as open up new avenues of thought for others to explore.*

will to put this into practice, and many will only make the change on a material level—this may be through their own actions, or the energy may manifest through the actions of others. Uranus cannot help but cause break-up where there is rigidity and prejudice, or unrecognized escapism and irresponsibility.

Uranus can bestow the ability to understand the hidden elements within life, from the viewpoint of the superconscious, but this can only occur when we let go of the ego's demanding needs which deny true changes: these may be psychological laziness, anger, dependency, helplessness, indecision, having fun, blaming other people and circumstances, and many other negative qualities which can assume a distorted importance, which deny true change.

> Life is or should be a constant, ongoing confrontation between yourself and the world, with an energy that keeps everything fresh and lively.[2]

This is how Uranus should be used: as a *constant, ongoing confrontation between yourself and the world.* Uranus in its more positive sense gives the ability to link in and understand *universal thought,* or in other words to have some understanding of universal symbolism. It can bestow certain gifts: nearly always there is some interest in astrology or the arcane. Though a positive aspect from Uranus sometimes may not be acknowledged or recognized for many years, as soon as the *will* of the individual links in with the Uranus energy a great deal can be achieved—if, of course, it is desired. Those with Uranus prominent can change themselves as well as open up new avenues of thought for others to explore.

Perhaps we are wrong if we believe that Uranus is not producing a logical thought process, for Uranus will link up thoughts so rapidly that they appear intuitive, and only when analyzed are shown to be completely logical in their outcome.

> Knowledge does not come to us by details, but in flashes of light from heaven.[3]

---

[2] Robert Hand, *Planets in Transit* (West Chester, PA: Whitford Press, 1976), p. 371.

[3] Henry David Thoreau, *The Natural Man, A Thoreau Anthology*, p. 79.

Uranus can allow us to realize that *all* thought processes that we experience come through planetary channels. A Greek philosopher once said that "even our thoughts are predestined," and anyone who studies the effects of transits on midpoints[4] will see that this statement is true.

Uranus gives the ability to observe and work with our thought processes—without becoming them—so that we develop more free will than we have hitherto enjoyed. Many of us think we have free will by always getting our own way, or by being different, but often the complete opposite is true. We have to find, and tread, our own pathway in life, and this can only be achieved through an understanding and uniting of our human natures.

In the *I Ching* or *Book of Changes,* it is found that the first number symbolizes The Creative, Heaven: above and below.

### THE CONDITION

The hexagram represents the primal power of Yang: light giving, active, strong, firm, of the spirit, energy unrestricted, durable. This power is expressed, first in the universe in the strong creative action of God and, second, in the human world in the creative action of the holy man or sage awakening and developing men's higher nature. . . . The Creative is made manifest only through the efforts of its activity.[5]

It goes on to say that Time is the instrument of the Creative. Through Time, the Creative moves, develops, transforms and shapes all in accordance with their true nature, keeping them conforming to the Great Harmony.

### THE IMAGE
The Creative, Heaven

As heaven moves with unceasing power,
So the wise man becomes strong, untiring.
Heaven upon heaven means duration
    both in and beyond time.

---

[4] The method devised by Reinhold Ebertin. For more details see his book *The Combination of Stellar Influences* (Tempe, AZ: American Federation of Astrologers, 1988).
[5] *The I Ching* or *Book of Changes,* trans. Richard Wilhelm (London: Arkana, 1984), p. 2.

As one day follows upon another in unending course,
    so the Creative never stops nor slackens.
Thus does the sage learn to develop himself
    so that his influence may endure.
Only by consciously limiting the field of one's activity
    can one attain tirelessness.[6]

Uranus symbolizes change, and change is certainly needed to really appreciate Uranus' incomparable properties: it is not just about "being different" and breaking rules, it is something far more precious and universal. Your ability to use the energy productively depends on just how free you are and whether your aims are for worldly excitement or inner wisdom. Ultimately the freedom that Uranus offers is the freedom that has its basis in *universal law,* for without this *law,* Uranus just becomes, at its best, a force for being different, and, at its worst, a rebelliousness that causes only havoc, breakdown, and destruction.

---

[6] *The I Ching* or *Book of Changes,* translated by Richard Wilhelm, p. 2.

# 17

# URANUS—WILL,
# FEELING, AND THOUGHT

> . . . The planets may be classified in terms of the three departments of human nature, action (will), feeling and thought. Some planets are stronger in one of these departments and others in another, but Uranus is remarkable for being equally strong in all three.
>
> —Alan Leo[1]

In Alan Leo's observation, we can see that perhaps the complex and manifold qualities that we encounter through Uranus are there due to the fact that they function on three different levels of consciousness, and while they may work in one person in a certain way, they may cause quite a different reaction from another.

If we look to see how Uranus affects our actions—or in other words our will—we see that this manifests more through aspects to the Sun, although Uranus in aspect to Mars, and Uranus positioned in the 1st and 5th house should also be noted. When it comes to will, the Uranian will is particularly strong and can be directed either at purely personal objectives, or linked in with universal aims; other factors in the chart will determine which, and sometimes both will operate together. In connection with will, Alan Leo comments:

> They find it difficult to work in a subordinate capacity, and are so independent that they do not easily co-operate with other people at all, even in a friendly way. They seem intended by

---

[1] Alan Leo, *The Art of Synthesis*, p. 95.

nature either for posts of authority and responsibility or for
venturesome and pioneering work. They are sometimes dis-
coverers, inventors and explorers: either actually in the outer
world around them or inwardly in the mental and moral worlds
where they formulate new rules, laws, methods, ideas, codes,
and opinions. They seldom keep to the beaten track, but prefer
to explore the unknown and to try new methods.[2]

To see how Uranus affects our feelings, we need to look at aspects to the
Moon. Uranus is perhaps less at home when connected to the
feelings,(unless, as with some of the more positive aspects between Uranus
and the Moon, they can operate on a more transpersonal level) because
emotional actions and reactions can be triggered by sudden and often irra-
tional tensions and impulses, which are formed from unconscious and
often negative behavior patterns learned in early childhood.

When it comes to the affections, Venus in difficult aspect to Uranus
can cause problems due to the wrong views, sudden infatuations, incom-
patibility and unconventional responses which are likely to occur. Even
the more positive aspects can cause difficulties at times, but the chart must
be looked at in its entirety for a more overall picture.

Uranus would seem most at home with Mercury. If Mercury represents the human mind, speech, and communication, then Uranus is the
inventive mind, astuteness, intuitive understanding, sudden cognition and
perception, and creative and original interpretation, although—particularly
with the hard aspects—the mind can be "flaky," and failures can occur
through nervousness, eccentric action, upset, and excitement.

All aspects of Mercury with Uranus denote an attunement of the
conscious, logical mind to the Universal Mind in some way;
but the harmony of the attunement should be noted. All of
these aspects indicate that the nervous system and the percep-
tions are speeded up to the point where the person can exhibit
great insight, ingenuity, originality, and memory; but the functioning of the mind tends to be erratic and undependable, especially where the aspects are challenging ones.[3]

[2] Alan Leo, *The Art of Synthesis,* p. 96.
[3] Stephen Arroyo, *Astrology, Karma & Transformation,* p. 120.

Those with natal aspects between Uranus and Mercury often have some interest in—or understanding of—astrology, and often communication between those with similar aspects is almost telepathic, so that a natural understanding immediately takes place; however one or more difficult aspects of Neptune to personal planets may cause some confusion as well.

When it comes to Thinking, you could say Mercury is an idea and Uranus an original or inventive thought, and both can be put into practice. There is nothing to say the idea has to be good, or kind or anything else, it is just an idea. Neither is there anything to say that any inventiveness or originality has to benefit the world: this, too, has to be decided by other factors within the chart.

If you see Mercury as the written word, and the intellect, linking words together as in thought and speech, then look to Uranus on the more inventive but material levels: here you find the invention of the word processor with its spell checkers; the now universal use of the computer which can store and regurgitate almost inconceivable amounts of information; television and video; satellite and telecommunication—in short, we can see space age integration of thought.

## URANUS—THE SELF AND THE PROMETHEUS MYTH

Some writers have suggested that Prometheus (the Higher Mind) is connected to the rulership of Aquarius, so it seems important to view their relationship. The Prometheus of mythology was said to give "fire" to physical creations. This fire, symbolic of the Sun, gave life to material existence; linked with the Higher Spiritual Sun, it is the "Spark of God" made manifest in human form. This spark is kept alive by the Spirit which issues from the Divine Sun.[4] The tarot card of The Hanged Man shows Prometheus (the Higher Mind) sacrificing himself on the altar of matter—or on the cross of material life—representing our own Higher Mind's descent into matter and all our earthly sufferings.

Prometheus is an appealing figure when seen as the personification of the unconquerable Will, and although chained and suffering, ultimately

---

[4] See *The Saturn/Pluto Phenomenon*, pp. 94-96.

*Universal power and the lightning flash which lifts our minds into that of God.*

triumphant of his cause. In order to understand the myth of Prometheus[5], it may be helpful to summarize briefly various factors within the mythological symbolism:

PROMETHEUS (the *Higher Mind*): It is said in esoteric philosophy that the *Higher Mind* (sometimes also called the soul) takes on earthly incarnations and, at the end of each earthly life, travels to another sphere or plane—often referred to as astral planes which are said to be above or below the earth—where it stays until its next incarnation. If the *Higher Mind* has risen above illusion and achieved liberation, it enters the realm of the Sun (the fourth realm above, where resides the *Pure Soul*) where incarnation is no longer a necessity, but a choice.

   *The Higher Mind*, while incarnating on earth, can be drawn upward to be influenced by the Higher Spheres and the *Soul*, the attunement of the *Higher Mind* with the *Soul* is referred to by some as the *Higher Self* or *Self*, and represents and expresses the Spiritualized Ego or Will. Likewise the *Higher Mind* can live in darkness, ignorant of the knowledge of its Divine origin, pulled down into matter by the influence of the *Lower Mind* (human mind, self, or lower self) which is made up from past desires, actions and reactions from previous incarnations; these are portrayed through the planetary channels as depicted on the natal chart.

   In *The Art of Synthesis*, Alan Leo says that Uranus is the planet for which the Sun was used as a substitute by those astrologers to whom the existence of Uranus was unknown. Its ideal, he says, is that of the king, regarded as gathering up in his own person all the different lines of activity in his kingdom.

   1) The Sun—Full self-consciousness. This—through the influence of the physical Sun and the "heart of the Sun"—produces awareness of the relation of the higher self and the lower self. Man becomes aware of his essential duality.

   2) Uranus—Occult consciousness or that intelligent, fusing condition which produces the scientific at-one-ment of the two

---

[5] See chapter 4 on Neptune.

factors, higher and lower self, through the intelligent use of the mind.

3) Neptune—Mystical consciousness or that innate sensitivity which leads unerringly to the higher vision, to the recognition of the inter-relation involved in man's essential duality during the process of manifestation, plus the activity of the mediator.[6]

The more we understand our human nature as depicted by the planetary influences, on all levels, the more we can unite both the material and the spiritual sides of our nature. Often when subjected to the inflow of strong transpersonal energies from Uranus, Neptune, or Pluto, the lower mind—the human ego—is unable to cope; in extreme cases, this may result in insanity, or intense religious fervor, or wanting to save the world, or any of the many other forms of lower mind delusion.

Until Uranus links with full Self-consciousness through Prometheus (the Higher Mind) the lightning flash of creative thought that lifts the mind into that of God cannot take place; for do we not see in the tarot card of The Fool the two sides of the Uranian influence—foolishness, but also wisdom? As the Higher Mercury, Uranus is the messenger who links in thoughts of the Universal Mind.

Uranus is the planet through which zodiacal energy flows, in connection with the Creative Hierarchies upon our planet. . .[7]

It is said consciousness is always expanding and the mind always opening up to new experiences, inventions, and consciousness. The role of Uranus is to bring in the new, to "awaken" human beings to new possibilities, which up to that time have been beyond immediate conception.

---

[6] Alice A. Bailey, *Esoteric Astrology* (New York & London: Lucis Press, 1951), p. 306.

[7] Alice Bailey, *Esoteric Astrology*, p. 99.

# APPENDIX 1

# QUESTIONS AND ANSWERS

> It is into the realm of symbols, of dreams, of myths and fairy tales, the domain of the shadowland, the kingdom of the idiot son and the imprisoned inner partner, that we must journey, marking our map as we go. And if one is too busy measuring how far one has gone, one may never know if and when one arrives.
>
> —Liz Greene[1]

QUESTION: Could you outline very briefly the best way to use the Saturn and Neptune meditations, plus the one connected to Pluto?

ANSWER: It is advisable to use the Saturn Meditation at regular intervals to begin with, gradually working toward an inner understanding of the necessity of Saturn's structure and form within your life. Then, after you begin to understand and gain strength from working with the Saturn Meditation, use the Pluto Meditation to look at, and let go of, old and outworn habits, desires and obsessions. When experiencing heavy transits and progressions from any planet, use the Saturn Meditation to give you strength to understand and work with the learning experience inherent at that time. The Neptune Meditation can be used whenever you feel the need to focus more upon your dreams and ideals, use this in conjunction with the Saturn Meditation to allow you to bring your dreams and ideals into more concrete reality, actuality, and existence, including all your more spiritual dreams and aspirations.

---

[1] Liz Greene, *Relating* (York Beach, ME: Samuel Weiser, 1973. London: Aquarian Press), p. 283.

QUESTION: I find imagery very difficult, does that mean I cannot do the meditations?

ANSWER: Some people will worry if they cannot "see" the images clearly. If this is the case, just feel and experience the different meditations and do not worry that you cannot see it all in complete clarity, try and allow yourself to just daydream. For instance, if someone told you to imagine a flower, a rose for instance, you would likely bring to mind a flower of a certain color and shape, you may also imagine what it smells like. Try and relax and see or feel the meditations in the same way.

QUESTION: Because of the confusing aspects of Neptune, isn't it impossible to work with this planet's influence?

ANSWER: If you do the Neptune Meditation as instructed, you will find it does help you to focus more on your own Neptune placement. Also by working with and understanding how important Saturn's influence is in your life, you start to ground your idealism on reality.

QUESTION: I understand that Neptune is connected to the astral planes. What is meant by the astral plane?

ANSWER: Esoteric philosophy speaks of Earth being positioned at the first point of seven astral planes or realms, both above and below it, each plane is ruled by a planetary Lord, or by the Lord of the Sun. The plane or sphere next to Earth possibly has conditions similar to our own. The 2nd and 3rd planes above and beyond would have an increasingly rarefied and heavenly atmosphere—although in these realms it is said illusion still remains—and little is known of those realms beyond and above the fourth. Likewise there are planes below the Earth encompassing negative conditions in differing and variable degrees. Men and women, while on earth, are thus capable of experiencing part of both upper and lower worlds simultaneously, and can through an act of Will reach up to the Divine, or else be pulled down into the depths of despair, deprivation, and even depravity. Pico della Mirandola, when quoting from Hermes Trismegistus,[2] said we

---

[2] Hermes Trismegistus is generally representative of every great saint, sage, and wise man of all ages. See G. R. S. Mead's *Thrice Greatest Hermes* (York Beach, ME: Samuel Weiser, 1992). Originally published in London in three volumes in 1906.

are positioned lower than the angels, higher than the beasts, and that every-thing depended on our own Will. We are also told that angelic or heavenly beings cannot walk the Earth or procreate, likewise the creatures of the ele-mental worlds cannot consciously enter into the Higher or Heavenly worlds. Only human beings can do both, as they possess an individual Soul, Higher Mind, and physical body.

QUESTION: How do you relate your theories about astrology to orga-nized religion, particularly Christianity?

ANSWER: The theories spoken of are first and foremost a search for Self-realization and are not related to any particular religion or creed. The search for Self-realization can never be based on a religious or social formula telling you how you *should* act, but upon a series of inner responsibilities for yourself, and your relationship to other people. In other words, you are not told by some outside body how to behave: all your actions are based upon an inner awareness which does not allow you to bring harm or impedi-ment to another. It is a philosophy which involves independence and free-dom for everyone to evolve along his or her own path, and can only be established through contact with one's own Soul.

QUESTION: Do you think that conditions like M.E. (*Imyalgic encephalitis*, also called post viral fatigue syndrome) are connected to planetary influ-ences, and if they are, what can we do about them?

ANSWER: I do believe that M.E. is connected to planetary influences. Almost all the charts I have seen of people suffering from M.E. have had exact, or almost exact, progressions of at least one of the outer planets (this means in particular the natal aspects of Saturn, Uranus, Neptune, and Pluto to each other, which have progressed to become exact or almost exact [within half a degree].) For example, look at the chart of Gabrielle who suffered M.E. more severely than anyone else I have ever known (see Chart 15, page 152). She trained as a social worker, and also had consid-erable talent as an artist. The first signs of M.E. appeared when she was in her mid-20s, growing steadily worse as time went by. From approximately 1986 to 1991 she was bedridden and almost completely unable to do any-thing for herself. Note the natal chart shows a Venus-Saturn-Neptune con-junction in Libra in the natal 12th house, Saturn and Neptune both square Uranus in the 9th house, and Neptune conjuncts the Ascendant.

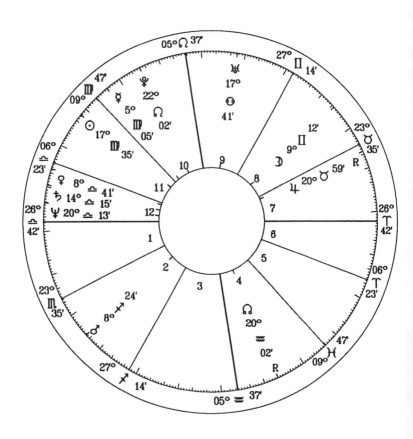

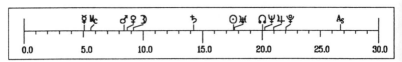

*Chart 15. Gabrielle's chart. Birth data from family has been withheld for confidentiality. Placidus houses. Chart calculated by Astrolabe using* Nova Printwheels.

In 1983, Gabrielle's progressed Sun was conjunct progressed Saturn (the conjunction with her natal Saturn occurred in 1979), and then moved on to square natal and progressed Uranus. She also had positive progressed aspects occurring from 1987-1988, including the progressed Sun sextile natal Pluto, and progressed Jupiter sextile Uranus (the Jupiter-Uranus sextile was in progress over several years).

Gabrielle's progressed chart shows that, during the period when she was severally ill (between 1986 and 1991), the progressed Sun was conjunct Neptune (natal and progressed); this progression was exact during 1986 and 1987, although the influence from this would have spread out over several years either way. (See Chart 16, page 154.)

During 1987, Gabrielle's progressed Venus squared natal Pluto, followed in 1988 by progressed Saturn square progressed Uranus (progressed Saturn was square natal Uranus in 1981), the duration of these progressed aspects would spread over several years, as would progressed Saturn moving toward a conjunction with natal Neptune. Note also that the progressed Ascendant is moving through the sign of Scorpio.

Gabrielle's chart is quite exceptional by the fact it has so many hard progressed aspects becoming exact, and it does illustrate how important these progressions are. Certain progressions are often missed, even by the most conscientious astrologer. Few books illustrate, or even mention, the importance of progressed aspects becoming exact, and although computer programs will pick up progressed aspects between the Sun, Moon, Mercury, Venus, Mars, and Jupiter to the outer planets, they do not all show any progressions occurring between the outer planets themselves. These are immensely important, particularly the more difficult progressions in their connection to physical and mental health. Obviously transits will also play an important role in the health of the individual, but because of the slower time factor, progressions should be noted first.

Since the middle of 1992, Gabrielle has been gradually improving, even if the progress is slow. The past few years have brought her near to death on several occasions, but she really feels that they have also given her time to think about the more spiritual aspects of her life, something she would not have felt she had time for had she been well. During 1992, the Sun progressed over her natal Ascendant into the 1st house, and although

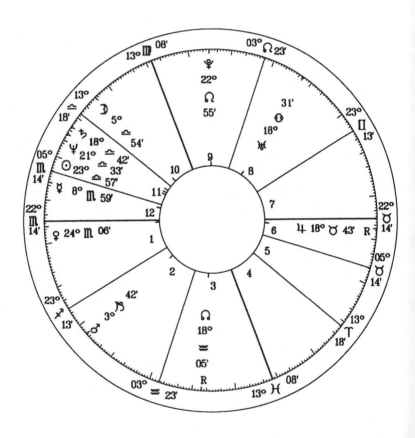

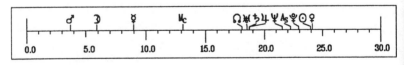

*Chart 16. Gabrielle. Progressed chart, 1989.*

the progressed Saturn-Neptune[3] conjunction is operative, progressed retrograde Jupiter is trine her Sun and exactly sextile progressed Uranus (this progression—although not exact—has been effective for several years); Gabrielle's progressed Mars trines natal Mercury.

QUESTION: You say there is no meditation connected to Uranus. How do we know we are working in harmony with this planet, and why can't we work with him in some sort of meditation?

ANSWER: By working with astrology and astrological symbolism you are working with Uranus, for Uranus gives the ability to understand and link together the mythic symbols within the universe. This may be by interpreting an astrological chart, or by using symbolic imagery in other ways, such as within the guided meditations.

QUESTION: It could be argued that, by exploring the depths of available literature we become aware of our individual paths; on the contrary, I believe that all the answers lie within and each is intuitively made aware in the natural progression of time and development to achieve the specific purpose of a particular incarnation. If more time was spent shutting out the bombardment of subjective material from the market place and instead spent listening to the inner voice, then the progress would be readily assured, and quicker.

ANSWER: I understand your concern regarding the market place, and we do have to choose wisely what we read, and yes, the answers do indeed lie within. However we need to be aware that a great deal of illusion exists in the human mind, and many of us need some guidance to understand and see beyond our own ego's demanding and often conflicting desires and condition. Each and every one of us needs to be sure exactly what our "inner voice" is, and where it comes from, for often it is no more than part of our human desire nature. By working with certain universal images, we begin to see things about ourselves it would be impossible to see entirely

---

[3] The exact progressed Saturn-Neptune aspect can be very debilitating in itself, causing difficulties with the immune system, water retention and sometimes severe weight gain. However, one of the greatest difficulties from this progression is in the depression which accompanies it, described by some as "the dark night of the soul."

through the intellect and its purely objective thought patterns. Until we know ourselves better, we are often washed about by life rather than learning from it, generating still more karma because of our as yet unconscious desires and actions.

QUESTION: Every so-called new age magazine is full of guidance from the market place, but, despite its so-called spiritual value, it is never freely given: Nirvana at a price, or whatever one fancies or happens to be the "in" workshop whereby one may achieve all that is desired to fill the vacuum left by the church and the old religions. It seems to me that some people are only out to make fortunes from their teachings.

ANSWER: There are, and always will be, many diverse people in the world seeking on many different levels of choice and experience, and each individual should be respected for his or her chosen path. The church was the panacea of the masses, and has to be replaced in some way or form, and there have been, and always will be, many traps for the unwary. The market place will harbor charlatans and knaves as it always has done, and the more escapist, glamorous and easy the message, the more likely it is to become popular. And, yes, many will make fortunes, if that is their over-riding desire and destiny. Luckily enough for those who can find it, there is also great inner wealth buried in many a simple word, and beauty, wisdom and truth do still exist. Plato believed that, although Absolute Truth could not be found through formulas, points of reference, or even mathematical rules showing the regularity of astrological bodies, through such knowledge we could come much nearer to the very Truth which we seek.

QUESTION: I have encountered many problems centering around the emotions and emotional relationships, but surely some mistakes are meant to be made. Are we not trying to change our destiny by avoiding them?

ANSWER: I'm sure we all make many mistakes. Eventually, however, there may come a point when we choose to understand just why we keep making the same mistake over and over again. Then, by working with the problem, we do start to change our destiny. However, even in starting to do this we are liable to make mistakes, due to the illusions of our own desire nature. By working with the meditations, and by accepting more responsibility for our own mistaken illusions, a greater balance starts to manifest within our life on Earth, and thus more understanding is generated.

QUESTION: I have tried many different techniques such as rebirthing and counseling, to liberate myself from emotional problems and to become more self-aware. What makes you think that the meditations may relieve certain problems where other therapies have seemed to fail?

ANSWER: Many people have counseling and take courses of all sorts, often hoping that by just doing so many long-standing and often deeply hidden and painful personality traits will be easily eradicated, or hoping that someone else will take on the responsibility for their problems. Unfortunately, it is not quite that simple. The aim of the meditations is to show you that the only way you can find release is by truly acknowledging your own shadow side. Also, by recognizing more the evasions and fantasies of your desire nature, you can begin to work with some of the causes of your past pain.

QUESTION: The new age of Aquarius is supposed to start around the year 1999. Could this be true?

ANSWER: When you are talking about ages that last around two thousand years each, it is more likely that the move from one age to another is a gradual process that may last some two or three hundred years in its entirety. However, it is likely that there is a period within those two or three hundred years when we are more under the influence of one age than the other.

QUESTION: As the Age of Pisces moves to the Age of Aquarius, can we expect many changes, and are these changes likely to be positive?

ANSWER: Many believe so, but no one really knows for certain exactly what the Age of Aquarius will bring. One thing we can do, is try to lift our consciousness, and make positive changes in our own personal worlds.

QUESTION: Is all the pain being experienced by so many in the world today karmic?

ANSWER: This is very likely, as karma is personal and collective, national, and of a worldwide nature. Karma is universal in its application, and is the law that "effect has to follow cause," or, in other words, that one's desires and actions automatically have repercussions, in this and future lives. No one is free from karmic law while on Earth; any deed perpetrated by the desire nature reaps its own karmic harvest.

QUESTION: Can you explain further?

ANSWER: We are told that karma is made from past desires, actions and reactions, and that it is the law of effect following cause. It is this action which eventually creates our destiny. Through great cycles of time our thoughts shape our lives through the patterns they weave, and the desires they generate.

QUESTION: Is it possible to understand and work with past karma?

ANSWER: Yes it is very simple, and at the same time very difficult. It can be developed by understanding our desires and actions on the deepest of possible levels through contact with the Self.

QUESTION: Can it help to be regressed back to past lives in order to understand our karma?

ANSWER: This in itself may create more illusion.

QUESTION: But it is possible to be regressed back to past lives while under hypnosis I believe?

ANSWER: Often what is experienced under hypnotic regression is more symbolic than actual past life memory, so try to keep an open mind. Many of the images may be grounded in past reality, but they may only symbolize something that occurred in a previous existence and now, in due time, have produced karma to work through. It is usually a mistake to take the images perceived too literally. Use them in relation to past lives by all means, but to see them as actual realities could be deluding you and leading you astray if you are not careful.

QUESTION: How is it that mythological figures represent the planetary energies?

ANSWER: These figures are the rulers of the elements from long, long ago. They were worshipped by the ancients and this has given them shape and form for us.

QUESTION: Can you explain more of what you mean by being governed by archetypal images?

ANSWER: The word archetype means an original model after which other similar things are patterned. For C. G. Jung they were symbolic mental images inherited by all of us from the collective unconscious (e.g., Earth Mother, Wise Old Man, God, Hero, the Child, Trickster, as well as many natural objects, such as Sun, Moon, Wind).[4] Although archetypes are separate structures in the collective unconscious, they can form combinations, and since the archetypes are capable of interacting with each other, they produce many personality differences among individuals. Used in an astrological context, it suggests that the mental images are determined by planetary positions and aspects; thus while symbolizing the main archetype they will also be experienced on a personal level by the individual. For example, consider a man's chart with the Moon conjunct Venus in Pisces in the 6th house both opposing Uranus and Pluto in Virgo in the 12th. This person's image may be of a compassionate caring mother, but one whom he also experienced as being erratic, unpredictable, devious, and controlling. This image in turn would be projected onto the women in his life. Unless the inner archetype were investigated, the same pattern would repeat itself, for each time and with each different woman the same image would eventually become his reality.

QUESTION: What is the point of working to understand what the planets mean in relation to our own minds?

ANSWER: If you think about my answer to the last question, you will see that by working to understand how the planetary influences affect our

---

[4] See C. G. Jung, *The Collected Works of C. G. Jung,* Vol. 9, *The Archetypes and the Collective Unconscious,* Bollingen Series XX, trans. R. F. C. Hull (Princeton, NJ: Princeton University Press, 1959), p. 4ff. Jung's ideas about archetypes are also presented in many anthologies of his work.

minds, we can learn to understand them and use them on a higher level of awareness. We can never completely erase them, for they are part of us, but by working responsibly and steadily to understand their meaning we can transform and transmute their influence. The planetary placing in the above example could indicate tremendous creative power that could be used in work and service to others, and which could bring about a significant inner healing, particularly  as the individual learned to work with his victim subpersonality.[5]

QUESTION: What is the difference between an archetype and a subpersonality?

ANSWER: To explain it in a very simple fashion, an archetype is an inherited symbolic image, while a subpersonality is an inherited character trait; you could also loosely describe a subpersonality as part of an archetype which we act out, rather than projecting onto someone else.

QUESTION: Can you see mental illness from a person's chart?

ANSWER: You can see certain difficulties, but it is necessary to define what "mental instability" actually is, for planetary positions or aspects can manifest in different ways in different charts. The outer planets—particularly in difficult aspect to personal planets—are the most likely to cause mental discomfort and unbalanced behavior at times. However, the more unconscious the individual, the more likely this instability will be. Also an unhealthy life style, too much drink, or drugs, may tip the balance the wrong way. The artist Vincent Van Gogh suffered greatly through mental instability and finally committed suicide, dying on July 29, 1890. See Chart 17 on page 162.

In Van Gogh's chart, a Cancer Ascendant shows a sensitive nature, and the Aries Sun and Mercury plus two planets in the 10th house suggests a need for attention and acclaim in the world (success came after his death, before then he sold only one painting). Mercury conjuncts Pluto, which in turn conjuncts Uranus (Uranus also makes a wide conjunction with Saturn),

---

[5] *The Saturn/Pluto Phenomenon;* see chapter on subpersonalities, and Pluto in the 12th house, pp. 133, 134.

perhaps causing very deep and uncontrollable thoughts. But similar combinations are found in the charts of many people who manage to live normal lives today, so one cannot help wondering if life would be any easier for Van Gogh were he alive now (many are using the energies from the transpersonal planets in a positive and transforming way), although the medical treatment of mental illness has not developed as one would have wished. His chart has positive indications, too, although the Moon is in a very wide square to Neptune, perhaps making him overly idealistic regarding emotional involvement (note that Saturn sectiles Neptune), the Moon also conjuncts Jupiter, and both trine Mercury suggests he was in touch with his feelings and was generous and kind in his thoughts, even overly optimistic at times. However, this Moon Jupiter conjunction in the 6th house squares a Venus-Mars conjunction in the 10th house, which may indicate some of the frustration he felt regarding his career and within certain intimate relationships.

At the time of Van Gogh's suicide, his progressed Sun had just gone over an exact conjunction of natal Saturn, and progressed Venus—although not exact—was near a one degree conjunction of progressed Sun and natal Saturn. Progressed Moon was in an exact conjunction of natal Pluto at the time of his death. These progressions all operating together would produce grave suffering, particularly in one so sensitive. Progressed Mercury trine the Moon was also within a one degree orb.

QUESTION: Are there any particular remedies you can recommend for working with difficult Saturn, Uranus, Neptune, and Pluto aspects, including transits and progressions?

ANSWER: Yes, there are several flower remedies which can be used successfully with any of the above planets, as well as individual remedies which will be dealt with separately. The general remedies are mimulus for fears of a known origin; aspen for unknown anxiety; rock rose for panic; St. John's wort to release deep fears—even those formed in past existences. Chestnut bud will help you learn from past mistakes so you do not continue repeating them; add cerato to this and it will help you also make the right decisions and stick to them (these two remedies taken together are very valuable). Vervain helps with varying degrees of tension; white chestnut will stop the mind going round and round without stopping. The gem remedies spoken of on pages 93-95 are extremely valuable for any long-term

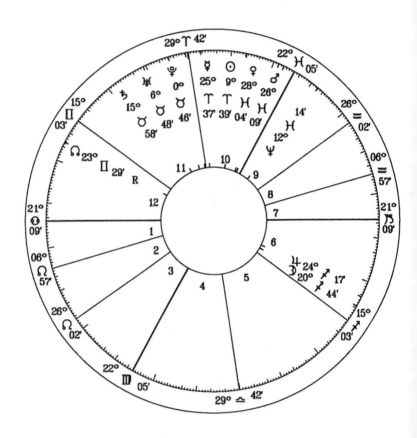

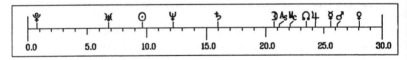

*Chart 17. Vincent Van Gogh's chart. March 30, 1853, 11:00 A.M. GMT. North Brabant, Netherlands. Data from* The Blackwell Data Collection, *published by Astrolabe.* Placidus houses. *Chart calculated by Astrolabe using* Nova Printwheels.

difficult transit or progression, particularly those that affect the Moon and Venus, and/or where Neptune and Pluto are involved. The gem remedies can help the chakras or energy centers from becoming blocked, and allow integration and positive growth in the area of inner and outer life which is affected. They can safely be mixed with any of the flower remedies.

**Saturn Remedies:** Difficult transits or progressions to personal planets by Saturn can cause you to feel overwhelmed by responsibility—this may be at home or at work—elm will give you the ability to cope with all you have to do (this is particularly good for those in the helping professions who feel they have no strength to go on supporting others). Saturn transits will often undermine your confidence, so sunflower will help balance your ego energies and give you the confidence to be yourself. If you lack self-worth, buttercup is the remedy. Gorse will help you to see things in a more positive light so that you do not always look on the black side of things. Add sweet chestnut if you also feel extreme anguish of thought. Pine will stop guilt and recrimination. Beech will help you to be more tolerant of yourself and others. Willow will stop bitter and resentful thoughts. Red chestnut is generally used where there is over concern for the welfare of others, but is also useful where there are inhibitions and shyness, because it stops the person concerned worrying too much about other people and what they may think of him/her. Also take note of the general remedies associated with fears and anxiety above.

**Uranus Remedies:** The homeopathic remedy arnica takes away the feeling of shock often felt during Uranus transits and progressions; this can also be taken in flower remedy form. The Bach combination rescue remedy is also useful for general unease, panic, and shock. Cherry plum helps with uncontrollable thoughts or actions, or the feeling of being out of control. Impatiens can help with irritability and impatience. Scleranthus is good if you find yourself swinging from one idea or extreme to another. If you are experiencing an extremely hectic life style, dill will enable you to slow down mentally and get details into perspective. Calendula will enable you to listen to other's words more easily.

**Neptune Remedies:** Clematis is useful for dreamy states which usually accompany a Neptune transit or progression. Rabbit brush can help focus the mind, and likewise madia can help where there is difficulty with details. All the remedies associated with fears, mentioned in the general section are useful, so is gorse for pessimism, also any of the remedies associated with despondency, such as gentian for depression of a known origin, sweet chestnut for extreme mental depression and anguish, mustard for a dark depressive cloud that comes and goes for no known reason, and hornbeam for that negative Monday morning feeling—good for those who have difficulty getting out of bed.

**Pluto Remedies:** The previously mentioned remedies for depression as well as the gem remedies—mainly gorse, gentian, sweet chestnut and mustard—really help with the long, slow transits of Pluto, and may be taken almost continuously throughout difficult periods. Vervain will alleviate some of the tension. Pluto is likely to bring certain fears to the surface, so the remedies for fear in the general section are good. Pluto often brings out emotional and related problems, and bleeding heart can release emotional attachments, allowing love to exist in freedom. Chicory helps with over possessiveness, holly with jealousy, envy and hate. Garlic can, in some people, release anxieties and insecurities which drain vitality. Vine will help if you are involved in power struggles with others.

QUESTION: Have you ever found people who could not do the meditations, and if so why?

ANSWER: Nearly everyone can do the meditations to some degree. Initially some may find it difficult to "let go," or their minds may wander, or they may have difficulty visualizing. However, all who truly want to work this way (and not everybody does) will find perseverance brings very rewarding results.

QUESTION: Can you say more on how the planets have both a positive and negative affect upon us?

ANSWER: Every planet has a positive and negative pole; you could say it is a matter of vibration. For instance Jupiter—the planet of growth and optimism—can, on a negative level, symbolize over-optimism and self-indulgence. Likewise Saturn's negative pole can represent restriction, limitations, and inhibitions, but the positive side is responsibility, wise caution, and the acceptance of hard work to reach the required goal on both inner and outer levels.

QUESTION: Can you use the Saturn Meditation on children?

ANSWER: Certainly, as long as the idea is explained to the child carefully and responsibility is taken for the child as he or she uses, the meditation; they can, like adults, use it to gain strength and to tackle their problems in a balanced and fair way (see page 78-79).

QUESTION: What if I have any difficulties when doing the meditation? For example, I found I could not understand what was shown me in either the Subpersonality or Neptune Meditations.

ANSWER: Take the problem to Saturn and work with it until you understand what you are being shown.

# Appendix 2

# TABLES

## SATURN POSITIONS 1900–2000 A.D.

| | |
|---|---|
| Jan. 1, 1900–Jan. 20, 1900 ........Sagittarius | Mar. 15, 1929–May 4, 1929 ......Capricorn |
| Jan. 21, 1900–July 18, 1900 ......Capricorn | May 5, 1929–Nov. 29, 1929 ......Sagittarius |
| July 19, 1900–Oct. 16, 1900......Sagittarius | Nov. 30, 1929–Feb. 23, 1932.....Capricorn |
| Oct. 17, 1900–Jan. 19, 1903......Capricorn | Feb. 24, 1932–Aug. 13, 1932.....Aquarius |
| Jan. 20, 1903–April 12, 1905 .....Aquarius | Aug. 14, 1932–Nov. 19, 1932 ....Capricorn |
| April 13, 1905–Aug. 16, 1905 ....Pisces | Nov. 20, 1932–Feb. 13, 1935.....Aquarius |
| Aug. 17, 1905–Jan. 7, 1906 .......Aquarius | Feb. 14, 1935–April 25, 1937 ....Pisces |
| Jan. 8, 1906–Mar. 18, 1908 .......Pisces | April 26, 1937–Oct. 18, 1937 ....Aries |
| Mar. 19, 1908–May 16, 1910 .....Aries | Oct. 19, 1937–Jan. 15, 1938......Pisces |
| May 17, 1910–Dec. 14, 1910 .....Taurus | Jan. 16, 1938–July 7, 1939 ........Aries |
| Dec. 15, 1910–Jan. 19, 1911 .....Aries | July 8, 1939–Sept. 23, 1939.......Taurus |
| Jan. 20, 1911–July 16, 1912 ......Taurus | Sept. 24, 1939–Jan. 20, 1940 .....Aries |
| July 17, 1912–Nov. 30, 1912 .....Gemini | Jan. 21, 1940–May 9, 1942........Taurus |
| Dec. 1, 1912–Mar. 25, 1913......Taurus | May 10, 1942–June 21, 1944 .....Gemini |
| Mar. 26, 1913–Aug. 24, 1914 ....Gemini | June 22, 1944–Aug. 3, 1946 ......Cancer |
| Aug. 25, 1914–Dec. 6, 1914......Cancer | Aug. 4, 1946–Sept. 20, 1948 .....Leo |
| Dec. 7, 1914–May 11, 1915.......Gemini | Sept. 21, 1948–April 4, 1949 .....Virgo |
| May 12, 1915–Oct. 16, 1916 .....Cancer | April 5, 1949–May 30, 1949 ......Leo |
| Oct. 17, 1916–Dec. 7, 1916 ......Leo | May 31, 1949–Dec. 31, 1949 .....Virgo |
| Dec. 8, 1916–July 23, 1917 .......Cancer | Jan. 1, 1950–Nov. 21, 1950.......Virgo |
| July 24, 1917–Aug. 11, 1919 .....Leo | Nov. 22, 1950–Mar. 7, 1951 .....Libra |
| Aug. 12, 1919–Oct. 7, 1921 ......Virgo | Mar. 8, 1951–Aug. 13, 1951......Virgo |
| Oct. 8, 1921–Dec. 19, 1923 ......Libra | Aug. 14, 1951–Oct. 20, 1953 ....Libra |
| Dec. 20, 1923–April 5, 1924 .....Scorpio | Oct. 21, 1953–Jan. 10, 1956......Scorpio |
| April 6, 1924–Sept. 13, 1924 .....Libra | Jan. 11, 1956–May 14, 1956 ......Sagittarius |
| Sept. 14, 1924–Dec. 2, 1926 .....Scorpio | May 15, 1956–Oct. 10, 1956 .....Scorpio |
| Dec. 3, 1926–Mar. 14, 1929 ......Sagittarius | Oct. 11, 1956–Jan. 5, 1959 .......Sagittarius |

## SATURN POSITIONS 1900–2000 A.D. (CONT.)

| | |
|---|---|
| Jan. 6, 1959–Jan. 3, 1962..........Capricorn | July 27, 1978–Sept. 21, 1980 .....Virgo |
| Jan. 4, 1962–Mar. 23, 1964 .......Aquarius | Sept. 22, 1980–Nov. 29, 1982....Libra |
| Mar. 24, 1964–Sept. 15, 1964 ....Pisces | Nov. 30, 1982–May 6, 1983 ......Scorpio |
| Sept. 16, 1964–Dec. 15, 1964 ....Aquarius | May 7, 1983–Aug. 24, 1983 ......Libra |
| Dec. 16, 1964–Mar. 3, 1967......Pisces | Aug. 25, 1983–Nov. 17, 1985 ....Scorpio |
| Mar. 4, 1967–April 29, 1969 .....Aries | Nov. 18, 1985–Feb. 13, 1988.....Sagittarius |
| April 30, 1969—June 18, 1971...Taurus | Feb. 14, 1988–June 10, 1988 .....Capricorn |
| June 19, 1971–Jan. 10, 1972......Gemini | June 11, 1988–Nov. 12, 1988 ....Sagittarius |
| Jan. 11, 1972–Feb. 21, 1972 .....Taurus | Nov. 13, 1988–Feb. 6, 1991 ......Capricorn |
| Feb. 22, 1972–Aug. 1, 1973 ......Gemini | Feb. 7, 1991–May 21, 1993 .......Aquarius |
| Aug. 2, 1973–Jan. 7, 1974 ........Cancer | May 22, 1993–June 30, 1993 .....Pisces |
| Jan. 8, 1974–April 18, 1974.......Gemini | July 1, 1993–Jan. 28, 1994 ........Aquarius |
| April 19, 1974–Sept. 17, 1975....Cancer | Jan. 29, 1994–April 7, 1996.......Pisces |
| Sept. 18, 1975–Jan. 14, 1976 .....Leo | April 8, 1996–June 9, 1998 .......Aries |
| Jan. 15, 1976–June 5, 1976 .......Cancer | June 10, 1998–Oct. 25, 1998.....Taurus |
| June 6, 1976–Nov. 16, 1977......Leo | Oct. 26, 1998–Mar. 1, 1999......Aries |
| Nov. 17, 1977–Jan. 5, 1978.......Virgo | Mar. 2, 1999–Dec. 31, 1999......Taurus |
| Jan. 6, 1978–July 26, 1978 ........Leo | |

## URANUS POSITIONS 1900–2000 A.D.

| | |
|---|---|
| Jan. 1, 1900–Dec. 19, 1904 .......Sagittarius | Jan. 28, 1956–June 9, 1956 .......Cancer |
| Dec. 20, 1904–Jan. 29, 1912 .....Capricorn | June 10, 1956–Oct. 31, 1961.....Leo |
| Jan. 30, 1912–Sep. 3, 1912........Aquarius | Nov. 1, 1961–Jan. 9, 1962 ........Virgo |
| Sep. 4, 1912–Nov. 11, 1912 ......Capricorn | Jan. 10, 1962–Aug. 9, 1962 .......Leo |
| Nov. 12, 1912–May 31, 1919.....Aquarius | Aug. 10, 1962–Sep. 27, 1968 .....Virgo |
| April 1, 1919–Aug. 15, 1919 .....Pisces | Sep. 28, 1968–May 19, 1969.....Libra |
| Aug. 16, 1919–Jan. 21, 1920 .....Aquarius | May 20, 1969–June 23, 1969 .....Virgo |
| Jan. 22, 1920–March 30, 1927 ...Pisces | June 24, 1969–Nov. 20, 1974 ....Libra |
| March 31, 1927–Nov. 3, 1927....Aries | Nov. 21, 1974–April 30, 1975....Scorpio |
| Nov. 4, 1927–Jan. 12, 1928.......Pisces | May 1, 1975–Sep. 7, 1975.........Libra |
| Jan. 13, 1928–June 5, 1934 .......Aries | Sep. 8, 1975–Feb. 16, 1981 .......Scorpio |
| June 6, 1934–Oct. 9, 1934 ........Taurus | Feb. 17, 1981–March 19, 1981 ...Sagittarius |
| Oct. 10, 1934–March 27, 1935...Aries | March 20, 1981–Nov. 15, 1981 ..Scorpio |
| March 28, 1935–Aug. 6, 1941 ....Taurus | Nov. 16, 1981–Feb. 14, 1988.....Sagittarius |
| Aug. 7, 1941–Oct. 4, 1941........Gemini | Feb. 15, 1988–May 26, 1988 .....Capricorn |
| Oct. 5, 1941–May 14, 1942.......Taurus | May 27, 1988–Dec. 1, 1988.......Sagittarius |
| May 15, 1942–Aug. 29, 1948 .....Gemini | Dec. 2, 1988–March 31, 1995 ....Capricorn |
| Aug. 30, 1948–Nov. 11, 1948 ....Cancer | April 1, 1995–June 8, 1995 .......Aquarius |
| Nov. 12, 1948–June 9, 1949 ......Gemini | June 9, 1995–Jan. 11, 1996 .......Capricorn |
| June 10, 1949–Aug. 23, 1955.....Cancer | Jan. 12, 1996–Dec. 31, 1999 .....Aquarius |
| Aug. 24, 1955–Jan. 27, 1956 .....Leo | |

## NEPTUNE POSITIONS 1900–2000 A.D.

| | |
|---|---|
| Jan. 1, 1900–July 18, 1901 ........Gemini | Dec. 24, 1955–March 11, 1956 ..Scorpio |
| July 19, 1901–Dec. 24, 1901 .....Cancer | March 12, 1956–Oct. 18, 1956...Libra |
| Dec. 25, 1901–May 20, 1902 .....Gemini | Oct. 19, 1956–June 14, 1957.....Scorpio |
| May 21, 1902–Sep. 22, 1914......Cancer | June 15, 1957–Aug. 5, 1957 ......Libra |
| Sep. 23, 1914–Dec. 13, 1914.....Leo | Aug. 6, 1957–Jan. 3, 1970 ........Scorpio |
| Dec. 14, 1914–July 18, 1915 .....Cancer | Jan. 4, 1970–May 2, 1970 .........Sagittarius |
| July 19, 1915–March 18, 1916 ...Leo | May 3, 1970–Nov. 5, 1970........Scorpio |
| March 19, 1916–May 1, 1916.....Cancer | Nov. 6, 1970–Jan. 18, 1984.......Sagittarius |
| May 2, 1916–Sep. 20, 1928 .......Leo | Jan. 19, 1984–June 22, 1984......Capricorn |
| Sep. 21, 1928–Feb. 18, 1929 .....Virgo | June 23, 1984–Nov. 20, 1984 ....Sagittarius |
| Feb. 19, 1929–July 23, 1929......Leo | Nov. 21, 1984–Jan. 28, 1998 .....Capricorn |
| July 24, 1929–Oct. 2, 1942 .......Virgo | Jan. 29, 1998–Aug. 22, 1998 .....Aquarius |
| Oct. 3, 1942–April 16, 1943......Libra | Aug. 23, 1998–Nov. 27, 1998 ....Capricorn |
| April 17, 1943–Aug. 1, 1943 .....Virgo | Nov. 28, 1998–Dec. 31, 1999 ....Aquarius |
| Aug. 2, 1943–Dec. 23, 1955......Libra | |

# BIBLIOGRAPHY

Arroyo, Stephen. *Astrology Karma & Transformation*. Sebastapol, CA: CRCS Publications, 1978.

Bach, Edward. *The Bach Flower Remedies*. See Nora Weeks.

————. *The Original Writings of Edward Bach*. Saffron Walden, Essex, England: C. W. Daniel Company, Ltd., 1990.

Bailey, Alice A. *Esoteric Astrology*. New York & London: Lucis Press, 1951.

Bhattacharya, A. K. *Gem Therapy*. Calcutta: KLM Private Ltd. May be obtained from the Flower and Gem Remedy Association. See under Resources.

Blavatsky, Madame. *The Secret Doctrine*. London: Theosophical Publishing House, 1893. Reprinted in 1980 by Theosophical Publishing House, Wheaton, IL.

Capra, Fritjof. *The Tao of Physics*. New York: Bantam, 1977.

Campbell, Joseph. *Creative Mythology, The Masks of God* series. New York & London: Penguin, 1976.

Carter, Charles. *The Astrological Aspects*. London: L. N. Fowler & Co., 1930.

*The Circle Book of Charts*. Compiled by Stephen Erlewine. Ann Arbor, MI: Circle Books, 1972.

*Classics of Western Philosophy*. Ed. Steven M. Cahn. Indianapolis, IN: Hackett Publishing Company, 1990.

Collins, Mabel. *Light on the Path*: *Through the Gates of Gold*. Pasadena, CA: Theosophical University Press, 1970.

Cronin, Vincent. *The Florentine Renaissance*. London: Pimlico, 1992.

Ebertein, Reinhold. *The Combination of Stellar Influences*. Tempe, AZ: American Federation of Astrologers, 1972.

Ferrucci, Piero. *What We May Be*. Wellingborough, England: Turnstone Press, 1982.

Ficino, Marsilio. *The Book of Life* (1948). Reprinted Dallas, TX by Spring Publications, University of Dallas, 1980.

*The Gem Remedy Directory*. Deddington, Oxon, England: The Flower and Gem Remedy Association. See under Resources.

Gibran, Kahlil. *The Prophet*. New York: Alfred A. Knopf, 1975.

Greene, Liz. *Relating*. York Beach, ME: Samuel Weiser, 1973; and London: Aquarian Press, HarperCollins, 1987.

————. *Saturn: A New Look at an Old Devil*. York Beach, ME: Samuel Weiser, 1976.

Hand, Robert. *Planets in Transit*. West Chester, PA: Whitford Press, 1976.

Harding, Michael, and Charles Harvey. *Working with Astrology*. London: Arkana, 1990.

Hebel, Doris. *Celestial Psychology: An Astrological Guide to Growth and Transformation*. Santa Fe, NM: Aurora Press, 1985.

Homer. *The Illiad*. Trans. E. V. Rieu. London: Penguin, 1964.

Jung, Carl. *Man and His Symbols*. New York: Dell, 1968; and London: Aldus Books, 1979.

Krishna, Gopi. *The Awakening of Kundalini*. Bombay, India: D. B. Taraporevala. Published under the auspices of the Kundalini Research Foundation, 1983.

————. *The Secret of Yoga*. Wellingborough, England: Turnstone Press, 1981.

Leo, Alan. *The Art of Synthesis*. Edinburgh: International Publishing Co., 1949. Reissued by Inner Traditions, Rochester, VT.

Lionel, Frederic. *The Magic Tarot*. London: Routledge & Kegan Paul, 1982.

Lundsted, Betty. *Astrological Insights into Personality*. San Diego: ACS Publications, 1980.

Machiavelli, Niccolo. *The Prince*. Trans. G. Bull. London: Penguin, 1970.

Maslow, Abraham. *Motivation and Personality*. New York: Harper and Row, 1970.

Mead, G. R. S. *Thrice Greatest Hermes: Studies in Hellenistic Theosophy and Gnosis*. York Beach, ME: Samuel Weiser, 1992. Originally published in London in three volumes in 1906.

————. *Pistis Sophia*. New York: Spiritual Science Library, 1984.

Michaud, Joy and Karen Hilverson. *The Saturn/Pluto Phenomenon*. York Beach, ME: Samuel Weiser, 1993.

Michelsen, Neil F. *Tables of Planetary Phenomena*. San Diego: ACS Publications, 1990.

Oken, Alan. *As Above, So Below*, included in Alan Oken's *Complete Astrology*. New York: Bantam, 1980.

Pagan, Isabelle M. *From Pioneer to Poet*. London: Theosophical Publishing Society, 1911. Reissued by Theosophical Publishing House, London, as *Signs of the Zodiac Analyzed*, 1978.

*The Penguin Book of Religious Verse*. Ed. R. S. Thomas. London: Penguin, 1963.

*The Republic of Plato*. Trans. John Llewelyn Davies and David James Vaughan. London: Macmillan and Co., 1897.

Sasportas, Howard. *The Gods of Change: Pain, Crisis and the Transits of Uranus, Neptune and Pluto*. London: Arkana, 1989.

*Six Centuries of Great Poetry*. Ed. Robert Penn Warren and Albert Erskine. New York: Dell Publishing, 1955.

Suzuki, Shunryu. *Zen Mind, Beginner's Mind*. New York: Weatherhill, 1985.

Tagore, Rabindraneth. "Unending Love," from *Selected Poems*. London: Penguin, 1985.

Thoreau, Henry David. *The Natural Man: A Thoreau Anthology*. Compiled by Robert Epstein and Sherry Phillips. Wheaton, IL: Theosophical Publishing House, 1978.

————. *Walden & Civil Disobedience*. London: Penguin Classics, 1986.

Waite, Arthur Edward. *The Pictorial Key to the Tarot*. York Beach, ME: Samuel Weiser, 1973.

Weeks, Nora. *The Medical Discoveries of Edward Bach, Physician*. Saffron Walden, England: C.W. Daniel, 1989.

Weeks, Nora and Victor Bullen. *The Bach Flower Remedies—Illustrations and Preparations*. Saffron Walden, England: C. W. Daniel, 1964.

Wilhelm, Richard. Trans. *The I Ching* or *Book of Changes*. London: Arkana, 1984.

# RESOURCES

1) Books by Madame H. P. Blavatsky may be obtained from your local metaphysical bookstore or you can write to the Theosophical Society's International Headquarters at the following address:

The Theosophical Society
P.O. Bin C
Pasadena, CA 91109

2) Visualization tapes of the following are available:

The Saturn Meditation

The Neptune Meditation

The Pluto Meditation

The Subpersonality Meditation

For prices and postage, write to Joy Michaud at the following address:

Joy Michaud
The Minster Centre
15 Silver Street
Ilminster
Somerset TA19 ODH
England

3) Bach Remedies—many health food stores now stock the Bach Flower Remedies; those who have no such source are recommended to contact one of the following for both remedies and books:

UNITED STATES
The Ellon Company
P.O. Box 320
Woodmere, NY 11598
Telephone: (516) 593-2206

UNITED KINGDOM
The Bach Flower Remedies
Unit 6
Suffolk Way
Abingdon
Oxon OX14 5JX
England
Telephone: 0235-550086; Fax 0235-523973

The Bach Centre
Mount Vernon
Sotwell
Wallingford
Oxon OX10 OPZ
England
Telephone: 0491-34678

CANADA
Bach Centre
P.O. Box 4265
Peterborough
Ontario, K9J 7Y8
Canada
Telephone: (705) 749-1894

GERMANY/AUSTRIA
Bach Centre German Office
M. Scheffer
Eppendorfer Landstr. 32
200 Hamburg 20
Germany
Telephone: 040-46-1041

AUSTRALIA
Martin and Pleasance, Ltd.
P.O. Box 2054
Richmond
Vic. 3121
Australia
Telephone: 427-7422

4) As well as the 38 remedies prepared by Dr. Bach in the 1930s, which are all marketed by the Bach Centre and its distributors, there are the Flower Essence Therapies that have been prepared mostly from North American plant species and have been available to the public since 1978. They are not replacements for Dr. Bach's work, but unique preparations in their own right. They are available from:

Flower Essence Services
P.O. Box 1769
Nevada City, CA 95959
Telephone: (916) 265-0258


5) Gem Remedies and Flower Remedies from around the world—including those from the Flower Essence Services; contact the following address for both remedies and books.

UNITED STATES
Alaskan Flower Essence Project
Box 1369
Homer, AK 99603-1369
Telephone: (907) 235-2188; Fax: (907) 235-2777

Pegasus Products
Box 228
Boulder, CO 80306
Telephone: 1-800-527-6104

UNITED KINGDOM
The Flower And Gem Remedy Association
Suite 1, Castle Farm
Clifton Road
Deddington
Oxon OX15 OTP
England
Telephone: 0869-737349; Fax: 0869-737376

# INDEX

Joy Michaud is a practicing psychotherapist, hypnotherapist, and astrologer. She gives lectures and holds workshops all over England, uniting her interests in astrology and psychology and demonstrating how people can connect with the mythic images within the unconscious in order to better understand the mind and personality. She is the co-author of *The Saturn/Pluto Phenomenon* also published by Samuel Weiser, and is currently working on another astrology book titled *The Mid-life Mystery*.

Erich Holmann, the artist of the eight black and white illustrations that appear in this book, worked extensively with the Uranus and Neptune meditations before creating this art. His drawings depict much of his own inner journey. Holmann's many paintings and drawings are in art collections throughout the world—including those of the Prince of Wales.